DATE DUE

DEMCO 38-296

ALGEBRA

SETS, SYMBOLS, AND THE
LANGUAGE OF THOUGHT

THE HISTORY OF MATHEMATICS

ALGEBRA

SETS, SYMBOLS, AND THE
LANGUAGE OF THOUGHT

John Tabak, Ph.D.

Facts On File, Inc.

ALGEBRA: Sets, Symbols, and the Language of Thought

Copyright © 2004 by John Tabak, Ph.D.

Permissions appear after relevant quoted material.

Facts On File, Inc.
132 West 31st Street
New York NY 10001

Library of Congress Cataloging-in-Publication Data
Tabak, John.
  Algebra : sets, symbols, and the language of thought / John Tabak.
    p. cm. — (History of mathematics)
  Includes bibliographical references and index.
  ISBN 0-8160-4954-8 (hardcover)
  1. Algebra—History. I. Title.
  QA151.T33 2004
  512—dc22 2003017338

Facts On File books are available at special discounts when purchased in bulk quantities for businesses, associations, institutions or sales promotions. Please call our Special Sales Department in New York at (212) 967-8800 or (800) 322-8755.

You can find Facts On File on the World Wide Web at http://www.factsonfile.com

Text design by David Strelecky
Cover design by Kelly Parr
Illustrations by Sholto Ainslie

Printed in the United States of America

MP FOF 10 9 8 7 6 5 4 3 2 1

This book is printed on acid-free paper.

To Diane Haber, teacher, mathematician, and inspirator.

CONTENTS

INTRODUCTION

ALGEBRA AS LANGUAGE

algebra *n.*

1. a generalization of arithmetic in which letters representing numbers are combined according to the rules of arithmetic

2. any of various systems or branches of mathematics or logic concerned with the properties and relationships of abstract entities (as complex numbers, matrices, sets, vectors, groups, rings, or fields) manipulated in symbolic form under operations often analogous to those of arithmetic

> *(By permission. From* Merriam-Webster's Collegiate Dictionary, *10th ed. © Springfield, Mass.: Merriam-Webster, 2002)*

Algebra is one of the oldest of all branches of mathematics. Its history is as long as the history of civilization, perhaps longer. The well-known historian of mathematics B. L. van der Waerden believed that there was a civilization that preceded the ancient civilizations of Mesopotamia, Egypt, China, and India and that it was this civilization that was the root source of most early mathematics. This hypothesis is based on two observations: First, there were several common sets of problems that were correctly solved in each of these widely separated civilizations. Second, there was an important incorrectly solved problem that was common to all of these lands. Currently there is not enough evidence to prove or disprove his idea. We can be sure, however, that algebra was used about 4,000 years ago in Mesopotamia. We know that some remarkably similar problems, along with their algebraic solutions, can be found on Egyptian papyri, Chinese paper, and

Mesopotamian clay tablets. We can be sure that algebra was one of the first organized intellectual activities carried out by these early civilizations. Algebra, it seems, is as essential and as "natural" a human activity as art, music, or religion.

No branch of mathematics has changed more than algebra. Geometry, for example, has a history that is at least as old as that of algebra, and although geometry has changed a lot over the millennia, it still *feels* geometric. A great deal of geometry is still concerned with curves, surfaces, and forms. Many contemporary books and articles on geometry, as their ancient counterparts did, include pictures, because modern geometry, as the geometry of these ancient civilizations did, still appeals to our intuition and to our experience with shapes. It is very doubtful that Greek geometers, who were the best mathematicians of antiquity, would have understood the ideas and techniques used by contemporary geometers. Geometry has changed a great deal during the intervening millennia. Still, it is at least probable that those ancient Greeks would have recognized modern geometry as a kind of geometry.

The same cannot be said of algebra, in which the subject matter has changed entirely. Four thousand years ago, for example, Mesopotamian mathematicians were solving problems like this:

> Given the area and perimeter of a plot of rectangular land, find the dimensions of the plot.

This type of problem seems practical; it is not. Despite the reference to a plot of land, this is a fairly abstract problem. It has little practical value. How often, after all, could anyone know the area and perimeter of a plot of land without first knowing its dimensions? So we know that very early in the history of algebra there was a trend toward abstraction, but it was a different kind of abstraction than what pervades contemporary algebra. Today mathematicians want to know how algebra "works." Their goal is to understand the logical structure of algebraic systems. The search for these logical structures has occupied much of the last hundred years of algebraic research. Today mathematicians who do research in the field of algebra often focus their attention on the mathematical structure of sets on which one or more abstract operations have been defined—operations that are somewhat analogous to addition and multiplication.

We can illustrate the difference between modern algebra and ancient algebra by briefly examining a very important subfield of contemporary algebra. It is called group theory, and its subject is the mathematical group. Roughly speaking, a *group* is a set of objects on which a single operation, somewhat similar to ordinary multiplication, is defined. Investigating the mathematical properties of a particular group or class of groups is a very different kind of undertaking from solving the rectangular-plots-of-land problem described earlier. The most obvious difference is that group theorists study their groups without reference to any nonmathematical object—such as a plot of land or even a set of numbers—that the group might represent. Group theory is solely about (mathematical) groups. It can be a very inward looking discipline. By way of contrast with the land problem, we include here a famous statement about finite groups. (A *finite group* is a group with only finitely many elements.) The following statement was first proved by the French mathematician Augustin-Louis Cauchy (1789–1857):

> Let the letter G denote a finite group. Let N represent the number of elements in G. Let p represent a prime number. If p (evenly) divides N then G has an element of order p.

You can see that the level of abstraction is much higher in this statement than in the rectangular-plot-of-land problem. To many well-educated laypersons it is not even clear what the statement means or even whether it means anything at all.

Ancient mathematicians, as would most people today, would have had a difficult time seeing what group theory, one of the most important branches of contemporary mathematical research, and the algebraic problems of antiquity have in common. In many ways, algebra, unlike geometry, has evolved into something completely new.

As algebra has become more abstract, it has also become more important in the solution of practical problems. Today it is an indispensable part of every branch of mathematics. The sort of algebraic notation that we begin to learn in middle school—"let x represent the variable"—can be found at a much higher level and in a much more expressive form throughout all contemporary mathematics. Furthermore it is now an important and widely utilized tool in scientific and engineering research. It is doubtful that the abstract algebraic ideas and techniques so familiar to mathematicians, scientists, and engineers can even be separated from the algebraic language in which those ideas are expressed. Algebra is everywhere.

This book begins its story with the first stirrings of algebra in ancient civilizations and traces the subject's development up to modern times. Along the way, it examines how algebra has been used to solve problems of interest to the wider public. The book's objective is to give the reader a fuller appreciation of the intellectual richness of algebra and of its ever-increasing usefulness in all of our lives.

1

THE FIRST ALGEBRAS

Mesopotamian ziggurat at Ur. For more than two millennia Mesopotamia was the most mathematically advanced culture on Earth. (The Image Works)

How far back in time does the history of algebra begin? Some scholars begin the history of algebra with the work of the Greek mathematician Diophantus of Alexandria (ca. third century A.D.). It is easy to see why Diophantus is always included. His works contain problems that most modern readers have no difficulty recognizing as algebraic.

Other scholars begin much earlier than the time of Diophantus. They believe that the history of algebra begins with the mathematical texts of the Mesopotamians. The Mesopotamians were a people who inhabited an area that is now inside the country of Iraq. Their written records begin about 5,000 years ago in the city-state of Sumer. The Sumerian method of writing, called cuneiform, spread throughout the region and made an impact that outlasted the nation of Sumer. The last cuneiform texts, which were written about astronomy, were made in the first century A.D., about 3,000 years after the Sumerians began to represent their language with indentations in clay tablets. The Mesopotamians were one of the first, perhaps *the* first, of all literate civilizations, and they remained at the forefront of the world's mathematical cultures for well over 2,000 years. Since the 19th century, when archaeologists began to unearth the remains of Mesopotamian cities in search of clues to this long-forgotten culture, hundreds of thousands of their clay tablets have been recovered. These include a number of mathematics tablets. Some tablets use mathematics to solve scientific and legal problems—for example, the timing of an eclipse or the division of an estate. Other tablets, called problem texts, are clearly designed to serve as "textbooks."

Mesopotamia: The Beginnings of Algebra

We begin our history of algebra with the Mesopotamians. Not everyone believes that the Mesopotamians knew algebra. That they were a mathematically sophisticated people is beyond doubt. They solved a wide variety of mathematical problems, some of which would challenge a well-educated layperson of today. The difficulty in determining whether the Mesopotamians knew any algebra arises not in what the Mesopotamians did—because their mathematics is well documented—but in how they did it. Mesopotamian mathematicians solved many important problems in ways that were quite different from the way we would solve those same problems. Many of the problems that were of interest to the Mesopotamians *we would solve with algebra*.

Although they spent thousands of years solving equations, the Mesopotamians had little interest in a general theory of equations. Moreover, there is little algebraic language in their methods of solution. Mesopotamian mathematicians seem to have learned mathematics simply by studying individual problems. They moved from one problem to the next and thereby advanced from the simple to the complex in much the same way that students today might learn to play the piano. An aspiring piano student might begin with "Old McDonald" and after much practice master the works of Frédéric Chopin. Ambitious piano students can learn the theory of music as they progress in their musical studies, but there is no necessity to do so—not if their primary interest is in the area of performance. In a similar way, Mesopotamian students began with simple arithmetic and advanced to problems that we would solve with, for example, the quadratic formula. They did not seem to feel the need to develop a theory of equations along the way. For this reason Mesopotamian mathematics is sometimes called protoalgebra or arithmetic algebra or numerical algebra. Their work is an important first step in the development of algebra.

It is not always easy to appreciate the accomplishments of the Mesopotamians and other ancient cultures. One barrier to our appreciation emerges when we express their ideas in our notation. When we do so it can be difficult for us to see why they had to work so hard to obtain a solution. The reason for their difficulties, however, is not hard to identify. Our algebraic notation is so powerful that it makes problems that were challenging to them appear almost trivial to us. Mesopotamian problem texts, the equivalent of our school textbooks, generally consist of one or more problems that are communicated in the following way: First, the problem is stated; next, a step-by-step algorithm or method of solution is described; and, finally, the presentation concludes with the answer to the problem. The algorithm does not contain "equals signs" or other notational conveniences. Instead it consists of one terse phrase or sentence after another. The lack of symbolic notation is one important reason the problems were so difficult for them to solve.

The Mesopotamians did use a few terms in a way that would roughly correspond to our use of an abstract notation. In particular they used the words *length* and *width* as we would use the variables x and y to represent unknowns. The product of the length and width they called *area*. We would write the product of x and y as xy. Their use of the geometric words *length*, *width*, and *area*, however, does not indicate that they were interpreting their work geometrically. We can be sure of this because in some problem texts the reader is advised to perform operations that involve multiplying *length* and *width* to obtain *area* and then adding (or subtracting) a *length* or a *width* from an *area*. Geometrically, of course, this makes no sense. To see the difference between the brief, to-the-point algebraic symbolism that we use and the very wordy descriptions of algebra used by all early mathematical cultures, and the Mesopotamians in particular, consider a simple example. Suppose we wanted to add the difference $x - y$ to the product xy. We would write the simple phrase

$$xy + x - y$$

In this excerpt from an actual Mesopotamian problem text, the short phrase $xy + x - y$ is expressed this way, where the words *length* and *width* are used in the same way our variables, x and y, are used:

> Length, width. I have multiplied length and width, thus obtaining the area. Next I added to the area the excess of the length over the width.
>
> *(Van der Waerden, B. L.* Geometry and Algebra in Ancient Civilizations. *New York: Springer-Verlag, 1983. Page 72. Used with permission)*

Despite the lack of an easy-to-use symbolism, Mesopotamian methods for solving algebraic equations were extremely advanced for their time. They set a sort of world standard for at least 2,000 years. Translations of the Mesopotamian algorithms, or methods of solution, can be difficult for the modern reader to appreciate, however. Part of the difficulty is associated with their complexity. From our point of view, Mesopotamian algorithms sometimes appear unnecessarily complex given the relative simplicity of the problems that they were solving. The reason is that the algorithms contain numerous separate procedures for what the Mesopotamians perceived to be different types of problems; each type required a different method. Our understanding is different from that of the Mesopotamians: We recognize that many of the different "types" of problems perceived by the Mesopotamians can be solved with just a few different algorithms. An excellent example of this phenomenon is the problem of solving second-degree equations.

Mesopotamians and Second-Degree Equations

There is no better example of the difference between modern methods and ancient ones than the difference between our approach and their approach to solving *second-degree equations.* (These are equations involving a polynomial in which the highest exponent appearing in the equation is 2.) Nowadays we understand that all second-degree equations are of a single form:

$$ax^2 + bx + c = 0$$

where *a*, *b*, and *c* represent numbers and *x* is the unknown whose value we wish to compute. We solve all such equations with a single very powerful algorithm—a method of solution that most students learn in high school—called the quadratic formula. The quadratic formula allows us to solve these problems without giving much thought to either the size or the sign of the numbers represented by the letters *a*, *b*, and *c*. For a modern reader it hardly matters. The Mesopotamians, however, devoted a lot of energy to solving equations of this sort, because for them there was not one form of a second-degree equation but several. Consequently, there could not be one method of solution. Instead the Mesopotamians required several algorithms for the several different types of second-degree equations that they perceived.

The reason they had a more complicated view of these problems is that they had a much narrower concept of number than we do. They did not accept negative numbers as "real," although they must have run into them at least occasionally in their computations. The price they paid for avoiding negative numbers was a more complicated approach to what we perceive as essentially a single problem. The approach they took depended on the exact values of *a*, *b*, and *c*.

Today we have a much broader idea of what constitutes a number. We use negative numbers, irrational numbers, and even imaginary numbers. We accept all such numbers as solutions to second-degree equations, but all of this is a relatively recent historical phenomenon. Because we have such a broad idea of number we are able to solve all second-degree algebraic equations with the quadratic formula, a one-size-fits-all method of solution. By contrast the Mesopotamians *perceived* that there were three basic types of second-degree equations. In our notation we would write these equations like this:

$$x^2 + bx = c$$
$$x^2 + c = bx$$
$$x^2 = bx + c$$

where, in each equation, b and c represent positive numbers. This approach avoids the "problem" of the appearance of negative numbers in the equation. The first job of any scribe or mathematician was to reduce or "simplify" the given second-degree equation to one of the three types listed. Once this was done, the appropriate algorithm could be employed for that type of equation and the solution could be found.

In addition to second-degree equations the Mesopotamians knew how to solve the much easier first-degree equations. We call these linear equations. In fact, the Mesopotamians were advanced enough that they apparently considered these equations too simple to warrant much study. We would write a first-degree equation in the form

$$ax + b = 0$$

where a and b are numbers and x is the unknown.

They also had methods for finding accurate approximations for solutions to certain third-degree and even some fourth-degree equations. (Third- and fourth-degree equations are polynomial equations in which the highest exponents that appear are 3 and 4, respectively.) They did not, however, have a general method for finding the precise solutions to third- and fourth-degree equations. Algorithms that enable one to find the exact solutions to equations of the third and fourth degrees were not developed until about 450 years ago. What the Mesopotamians discovered instead were methods for developing *approximations* to the solutions. From a practical point of view an accurate approximation is usually as good as an exact solution, but from a mathematical point of view the two are quite different. The distinctions that we make between exact and approximate solutions were not important to the Mesopotamians. They seemed completely satisfied as long as their approximations were accurate enough for the applications that they had in mind.

The Mesopotamians and Indeterminate Equations

In modern notation an indeterminate equation—that is, an equation with many different solutions—is usually easy to recognize. If we have one equation and more than one unknown then the equation is generally indeterminate. For the Mesopotamians geometry was a source of indeterminate equations. One of the most famous examples of an indeterminate equation from Mesopotamia can be expressed in our notation as

$$x^2 + y^2 = z^2$$

The fact that that we have three variables but only one equation is a good indicator that this equation is indeterminate. And so it is. Geometrically we can interpret this equation as the Pythagorean theorem, which states that for a right triangle the square of the length of the hypotenuse

Cuneiform tablet, Plimpton 322. This tablet is the best known of all Mesopotamian mathematical tablets; its meaning is still a subject of scholarly debate. (Plimpton 322, Rare Book and Manuscript Library, Columbia University)

CLAY TABLETS AND ELECTRONIC CALCULATORS

The positive square root of the positive number a—usually written as $\sqrt{a}$—is the positive number with the property that if we multiply it by itself we obtain a. Unfortunately, writing the square root of a as $\sqrt{a}$ does not tell us what the number is. Instead, it tells us what $\sqrt{a}$ does: If we square $\sqrt{a}$ we get a.

Some square roots are easy to write. In these cases the square root sign, $\sqrt{\ }$, is not really necessary. For example, 2 is the square root of 4, and 3 is the square root of 9. In symbols we could write $2 = \sqrt{4}$ and $3 = \sqrt{9}$ but few of us bother.

Calculator. Many electronic calculators use the square root algorithm pioneered by the Mesopotamians. (CORBIS)

The situation is a little more complicated, however, when we want to know the square root of 2, for example. How do we find the square root of 2? It is not an especially easy problem to solve. It is, however, equivalent to finding the solution of the second-degree equation

$$x^2 - 2 = 0$$

Notice that when the number $\sqrt{2}$ is substituted for x in the equation we obtain a true statement. Unfortunately, this fact does not convey much information about the size of the number we write as $\sqrt{2}$.

The Mesopotamians developed an algorithm for computing square roots that yields an accurate approximation for any positive square

(here represented by z^2) equals the sum of the squares of the lengths of the two remaining sides. The Mesopotamians knew this theorem long before the birth of Pythagoras, however, and their problem texts are replete with exercises involving what we call the Pythagorean theorem.

root. (As the Mesopotamians did, we will consider only positive square roots.) For definiteness, we will apply the method to the problem of calculating √2.

The Mesopotamians used what we now call a recursion algorithm to compute square roots. A recursion algorithm consists of several steps. The output of one step becomes the input for the next step. The more often one repeats the process—that is, the more steps one takes—the closer one gets to the exact answer. To get started, we need an "input" for the first step in our algorithm. We can begin with a guess; they did. Almost any guess will do. After we input our initial guess we just repeat the process over and over again until we are as close as we want to be. In a more or less modern notation we can represent the Mesopotamian algorithm like this:

$$OUTPUT = 1/2(INPUT + 2/INPUT)$$

(If we wanted to compute √5, for example, we would only have to change 2/INPUT into 5/INPUT. Everything else stays the same.)

If, at the first step, we use 1.5 as our input, then our output is $1.41\bar{6}$ because

$$1.41\bar{6} = 1/2(1.5 + 2/1.5)$$

At the end of the second step we would have

$$1.414215\ldots = 1/2(1.41\bar{6} + 2/1.41\bar{6})$$

as our estimate for √2. We could continue to compute more steps in the algorithm, but after two steps (and with the aid of a good initial guess) our approximation agrees with the actual value of √2 up to the millionth place—an estimate that is close enough for many practical purposes.

What is especially interesting about this algorithm from a modern point of view is that it is probably the one that your calculator uses to compute square roots. The difference is that instead of representing the algorithm on a clay tablet, the calculator represents the algorithm on an electronic circuit! This algorithm is as old as civilization.

The Pythagorean theorem is usually encountered in high school or junior high in a problem in which the length of two sides of a right triangle are given and the student has to find the length of the third side. The Mesopotamians solved problems like this as well, but the indeterminate form of the problem—with its three

unknowns rather than one—is a little more challenging. The indeterminate version of the problem consists of identifying what we
now call Pythagorean triples. These are solutions to the equation
given here that involve only whole numbers.

There are infinitely many Pythagorean triples, and Mesopotamian
mathematicians exercised considerable ingenuity and mathematical
sophistication in finding solutions. They then compiled these whole
number solutions in tables. Some simple examples of Pythagorean
triples include (3, 4, 5) and (5, 12, 13), where in our notation, taken
from a preceding paragraph, $z = 5$ in the first triple and $z = 13$ in the
next triple. (The numbers 3 and 4 in the first triple, for example, can
be placed in either of the remaining positions in the equation and the
statement remains true.)

The Mesopotamians did not indicate the method that they used
to find these Pythagorean triples, so we cannot say for certain how
they found these triples. Of course a few correct triples could be
attributed to lucky guesses. We can be sure, however, that the
Mesopotamians had a general method worked out because their
other solutions to the problem of finding Pythagorean triples
include (2,700, 1,771, 3,229), (4,800, 4,601, 6,649), and (13,500,
12,709, 18,541).

The search for Pythagorean triples occupied mathematicians in
different parts of the globe for millennia. A very famous generalization of the equation we use to describe Pythagorean triples was proposed by the 17th-century French mathematician Pierre de Fermat.
His conjecture about the nature of these equations, called Fermat's
last theorem, occupied the attention of mathematicians right up to
the present time and was finally solved only recently; we will describe
this generalization later in this volume. Today the mathematics for
generating all Pythagorean triples is well known but not especially
easy to describe. That the mathematicians in the first literate culture
in world history should have solved the problem is truly remarkable.

Egyptian Algebra

Little is left of Egyptian mathematics. The primary sources are a
few papyri, the most famous of which is called the Ahmes papyrus,

The Ahmes papyrus, also known as the Rhind papyrus, contains much of what is known about ancient Egyptian mathematics. (© The British Museum)

and the first thing one notices about these texts is that the Egyptians were not as mathematically adept as their neighbors and contemporaries the Mesopotamians—at least there is no indication of a higher level of attainment in the surviving records. It would be tempting to concentrate exclusively on the Mesopotamians, the Chinese, and the Greeks as sources of early algebraic thought. We include the Egyptians because Pythagoras, who is an important figure in our story, apparently received at least some of his mathematical education in Egypt. So did Thales, another very early and very important figure in Greek mathematics. In addition, certain other peculiar characteristics of Egyptian mathematics, especially their penchant for writing all fractions as sums of what are called unit fractions, can be found in several cultures throughout the region and even as far away as China. (A *unit fraction* is a fraction with a 1 in the numerator.) None of these commonalities proves that Egypt was the original source of a lot of commonly held mathematical ideas and practices, but there are indications that this is true. The Greeks, for example, claimed that their mathematics originated in Egypt.

Egyptian arithmetic was considerably more primitive than that of their neighbors the Mesopotamians. Even multiplication was not treated in a general way. To multiply two numbers together they used a method that consisted of repeatedly doubling one of the numbers and then adding together some of the intermediate steps. For example, to compute 5×80, first find 2×80 and then double the result to get 4×80. Finally, 1×80 would be added to 4×80 to get the answer, 5×80. This method, though it works, is awkward.

Egyptian algebra employed the symbol *heap* for the unknown. Problems were phrased in terms of "heaps" and then solved. To paraphrase a problem taken from the most famous of Egyptian mathematical texts, the Ahmes papyrus: If 1 heap and 1/7 of a heap together equal 19, what is the value of the heap? (In our notation we would write the corresponding equation as $x + x/7 = 19$.) This type of problem yields what we would call a linear equation. It is not the kind of exercise that attracted much attention from Mesopotamian mathematicians, who were concerned with more difficult problems, but the Egyptians apparently found them challenging enough to be worth studying.

What is most remarkable about Egyptian mathematics is that it seemed to be adequate for the needs of the Egyptians for thousands of years. Egyptian culture is famous for its stunning architecture and its high degree of social organization and stability. These were tremendous accomplishments, and yet the Egyptians seem to have accomplished all of this with a very simple mathematical system, a system with which they were apparently quite satisfied.

Chinese Algebra

The recorded history of Chinese mathematics begins in the Han dynasty, a period that lasted from 206 B.C.E. until 220 C.E. Records from this time are about 2,000 years younger than many Mesopotamian mathematics texts. What we find in these earliest of records of Chinese mathematics is that Chinese mathematicians had already developed an advanced mathematical culture. It would be interesting to know when the Chinese began to develop their mathematics and how their ideas changed over time, but little is known about mathematics in China before the founding of the Han dynasty. This lack of knowledge is the result of a deliberate act. The first emperor of China, Qin Shi Huang, who died in the year 210 B.C.E., ordered that all books be burned. This was done. The book burners were diligent. As a consequence, little information is available about Chinese mathematical thought before 206 B.C.E.

One of the first and certainly the most important of all early Chinese mathematical texts is *Nine Chapters on the Mathematical Art*, or the *Nine Chapters* for short. (It is also known as *Arithmetic in Nine Sections*.) The mathematics in the *Nine Chapters* is already fairly sophisticated, comparable with the mathematics of Mesopotamia. The *Nine Chapters* has more than one author and is based on a work that survived, at least in part, the book burning campaign of the emperor Qin Shi Huang. Because it was extensively rewritten and enlarged knowing what the original text was like is difficult. In any case, because the book was rewritten during the Han dynasty, it is one of the earliest extant Chinese mathematical texts. It is also one of the best known. It was used as a math text for generations, and it has served as an important source of inspiration for Chinese mathematicians.

In its final form the *Nine Chapters* consists of 246 problems on a wide variety of topics. There are problems in taxation, surveying, engineering, and geometry and methods of solution for determinate and indeterminate equations alike. The tone of the text is much more conversational than that adopted by the Mesopotamian scribes. It is a nice example of what is now known as rhetorical algebra. (*Rhetorical algebra* is algebra that is expressed with little or no specialized algebraic notation.) Everything—the problem, the solution, and the algorithm that is used to obtain the solution—is expressed in words and numbers, not in mathematical symbols. There are no "equals" signs, no x's to represent unknowns, and none of the other notational tools that we use when we study algebra. Most of us do not recognize what a great advantage algebraic notation is until after we read problems like those in the *Nine Chapters*. These problems make for fairly difficult reading for the modern reader precisely because they are expressed without the algebraic symbolism to which we have become accustomed. Even simple problems require a lot of explanatory prose when they are written without algebraic notation. The authors of the *Nine Chapters* did not shy away from using as much prose as was required.

Aside from matters of style, Mesopotamian problem texts and the *Nine Chapters* have a lot in common. There is little in the way of a general theory of mathematics in either one. Chinese and Mesopotamian authors are familiar with many algorithms that work, but they express little interest in *proving* that the algorithms work as advertised. It is not clear why this is so. Later Mesopotamian mathematicians, at least, had every opportunity to become familiar with Greek mathematics, in which the idea of proof was central. The work of their Greek contemporaries had little apparent influence on the Mesopotamians. Some historians believe that there was also some interaction between the Chinese and Greek cultures, if not direct then at least by way of India. If this was the case, then Chinese mathematics was not overly influenced by contact with the Greeks, either. Perhaps the Chinese approach to mathematics was simply a matter of taste. Perhaps Chinese mathematicians (and their Mesopotamian counterparts) had little interest in exploring the mathematical landscape in the way that the Greeks did. Or perhaps the Greek approach was unknown to the authors of the *Nine Chapters*.

Another similarity between Mesopotamian and Chinese mathematicians lay in their use of approximations. As the Mesopotamians did and the Greeks did not, Chinese mathematicians made little distinction between exact results and good approximations. And as their Mesopotamian counterparts did, Chinese mathematicians developed a good deal of skill in obtaining accurate approximations for square roots. Even the method of conveying mathematical knowledge used by the authors of the *Nine Chapters* is similar to that of the Mesopotamian scribes in their problem texts. Like the Mesopotamian texts, the *Nine Chapters* is written as a straightforward set of problems. The problems are stated, as are the solutions, and an algorithm or "rule" by which the reader can solve the given problem for himself or herself is described. There is little apparent concern for the foundations of the subject. The mathematics in the *Nine Chapters* is not higher mathematics in a modern sense; it is, instead, a highly developed example of "practical" mathematics.

The authors of the *Nine Chapters* solved many determinate equations (see the sidebar Rhetorical Algebra for an example). They were at home manipulating positive whole numbers, fractions, and even negative numbers. Unlike the Mesopotamians, the Chinese accepted the existence of negative numbers and were willing to work with negative numbers to obtain solutions to the problems that interested them. In fact, the *Nine Chapters* even gives rules for dealing with negative numbers. This is important because negative numbers can arise during the process of solving many different algebraic problems even when the final answers are positive. When one refuses to deal with negative numbers, one's work becomes much harder. In this sense the Chinese methods for solving algebraic equations were more adaptable and "modern" than were the methods used by the Mesopotamians, who strove to avoid negative numbers.

In addition to their work on determinate equations, Chinese mathematicians had a deep and abiding interest in indeterminate equations, equations for which there are more unknowns than there are equations. As were the Mesopotamians, Chinese mathematicians were also familiar with the theorem of Pythagoras and used the equation (which we might write as $x^2 + y^2 = z^2$) to pose indeterminate as well as determinate problems. They enjoyed finding Pythagorean triples just as the Mesopotamians did, and they compiled their results just as the Mesopotamians did.

The algebras that developed in the widely separated societies described in this chapter are remarkably similar. Many of the problems that were studied are similar. The approach to problem solving—the emphasis on algorithms rather than a theory of equations—was a characteristic that all of these cultures shared. Finally,

RHETORICAL ALGEBRA

The following problem is an example of Chinese rhetorical algebra taken from the *Nine Chapters*. This particular problem is representative of the types of problems that one finds in the *Nine Chapters;* it is also a good example of rhetorical algebra, which is algebra that is expressed without specialized algebraic notation.

In this problem the authors of the *Nine Chapters* consider three types or "classes" of corn measured out in standard units called measures. The corn in this problem, however, is not divided into measures; it is divided into "bundles." The number of measures of corn in one bundle depends on the class of corn considered. The goal of the problem is to discover how many measures of corn constitute one bundle for each class of corn. The method of solution is called the Rule. Here are the problem and its solution:

> There are three classes of corn, of which three bundles of the first class, two of the second and one of the third make 39 measures. Two of the first, three of the second and one of the third make 34 measures. And one of the first, two of the second and three of the third make 26 measures. How many measures of grain are contained in one bundle of each class?
>
> Rule. Arrange the 3, 2, and 1 bundles of the three classes and the 39 measures of their grains at the right.
>
> Arrange other conditions at the middle and at the left. With the first class in the right column multiply currently the middle column, and directly leave out.
>
> Again multiply the next, and directly leave out.
>
> Then with what remains of the second class in the middle column, directly leave out.
>
> Of the quantities that do not vanish, make the upper the *fa,* the divisor, and the lower the *shih,* the dividend, i.e., the dividend for the third class.
>
> To find the second class, with the divisor multiply the measure in the middle column and leave out of it the dividend for the third class. The remainder, being divided by the number of bundles of the second class, gives the dividend for the third class. To find the second class, with the divisor multiply the measure in the middle column and leave out of it the dividend for the third class. The remainder, being divided by the number of bundles of the second class, gives the dividend for the second class.

To find the first class, also with the divisor multiply the measures in the right column and leave out from it the dividends for the third and second classes. The remainder, being divided by the number of bundles of the first class, gives the dividend for the first class.

Divide the dividends of the three classes by the divisor, and we get their respective measures.

(*Mikami, Yoshio*. The Development of Mathematics in China and Japan. *New York: Chelsea Publishing, 1913*)

The problem, which is the type of problem often encountered in junior high or high school algebra classes, is fairly difficult to read, but only because the problem—and especially the solution—are expressed rhetorically. In modern algebraic notation we would express the problem with three variables. Let x represent a bundle for the first class of corn, y represent a bundle for the second class of corn, and z represent a bundle for the third class of corn. In our notation the problem would be expressed like this:

$$3x + 2y + z = 39$$
$$2x + 3y + z = 34$$
$$x + 2y + 3z = 26$$

The answer is correctly given as 9 1/4 measures of corn in the first bundle, 4 1/4 measures of corn in the second bundle, and 2 3/4 measures of grain in the third bundle.

Today this is not a particularly difficult problem to solve, but at the time that the *Nine Chapters* was written this problem was for experts only. The absence of adequate symbolism was a substantial barrier to mathematical progress.

not one of the cultures developed a specialized set of algebraic symbols to express their ideas. All these algebras were rhetorical. There was one exception, however. That was the algebra that was developed in ancient Greece.

2

GREEK ALGEBRA

Greek mathematics is fundamentally different from the mathematics of Mesopotamia and China. The unique nature of Greek mathematics seems to have been present right from the outset in the work of Thales of Miletus (ca. 625 B.C.E.–ca. 546 B.C.E.) and Pythagoras of Samos (ca. 582 B.C.E.–ca. 500 B.C.E.). In the beginning, however, the Greeks were not solving problems that were any harder than those of the Mesopotamians or the Chinese. In fact, the Greeks were not interested in problem solving at all—at least not in the sense that the Mesopotamian and Chinese mathematicians were. Greek mathematicians for the most part did not solve problems in taxation, surveying, or the division of food. They were interested, instead, in questions about the nature of number and form.

It could be argued that Chinese and Mesopotamian mathematicians were not really interested in these applications, either—that they simply used practical problems to express their mathematical insights. Perhaps they simply preferred to express their mathematical ideas in practical terms. Perhaps, as it was for their Greek counterparts, it was the mathematics and not the applications that provided them with their motivation. Though possible, this explanation is not entirely certain from their writings.

There is, however, no doubt about how the Greeks felt about utilitarian mathematics. The Greeks did not—would not—express their mathematical ideas through problems involving measures of corn or the division of estates or any other practical language. They must have known, just as the Mesopotamian and Chinese mathematicians knew, that all of these fields are rich sources of mathematical problems. To the Greeks this did not matter. The Greeks were interested in mathematics for the sake of mathematics. They expressed their ideas in terms of the properties of numbers, points, curves, planes, and geometric solids. Most of them had no interest in applications of their subject, and in case anyone missed the point they were fond of reciting the story about the mathematician Euclid of Alexandria, who, when a student inquired about the utility of mathematics, instructed his servant to give the student a few coins so that he could profit from his studies. There are other similar stories about other Greek mathematicians. Greek mathematicians were the first of the "pure" mathematicians.

Another important difference between Greek mathematicians and the mathematicians of other ancient cultures was the distinction that the Greeks made between exact and approximate results. This distinction is largely absent from other mathematical cultures of the time. In a practical sense, exact results are generally no more useful than good approximations. Practical problems involve measurements, and measurements generally involve some uncertainty. For example, when we measure the length of a line segment our measurement removes some of our uncertainty about the "true" length of the segment, but some uncertainty remains. This uncertainty is our margin of error. Although we can further reduce our uncertainty with better measurements or more sophisticated measurement techniques, we cannot eliminate all uncertainty. As a consequence, any computations that depend on this measurement must also reflect our initial imprecision about the length of the segment. Our methods may be exact in the sense that if we had exact data then our solution would be exact as well. Unfortunately, exact measurements are generally not available.

The Greek interest in precision influenced not only the way they investigated mathematics; it also influenced what they investigated. It was their interest in exact solutions that led to one of the most profound discoveries in ancient mathematics.

The Discovery of the Pythagoreans

Pythagoras of Samos was one of the first Greek mathematicians. He was extremely influential, although, as we will soon see, we cannot attribute any particular discoveries to him. As a young man Pythagoras is said to have traveled widely. He apparently received his mathematics education in Egypt and Mesopotamia. He may have traveled as far east as India. Eventually he settled on the southeastern coast of what is now Italy in the Greek city of Cortona. (Although we tend to think of Greek civilization as situated within the boundaries of present-day Greece, there was a time when Greek cities were scattered throughout a much larger area along the Mediterranean Sea.)

Pythagoras was a mystic as well as a philosopher and mathematician. Many people were attracted to him personally as well as to his ideas. He founded a community in Cortona where he and his many disciples lived communally. They shared property, ideas, and credit for those ideas. No Pythagorean took individual credit for a discovery, and as a consequence we cannot be sure which of the discoveries attributed to Pythagoras were his and which were his disciples'. For that reason we discuss the contributions of the Pythagoreans rather than the contributions of Pythagoras himself. There is, however, one point about Pythagoras about which we can be sure: Pythagoras did not discover the Pythagorean theorem. The theorem was known to Mesopotamian mathematicians more than 30 generations before Pythagoras's birth.

At the heart of Pythagorean philosophy was the maxim "All is number." There is no better example of this than their ideas about music. They noticed that the musical tones produced by a string could be described by whole number ratios. They investigated music with an instrument called a monochord, a device consisting of one string stretched between two supports. (The supports may have been attached to a hollow box to produce a richer, more harmonious sound.) The Pythagorean monochord

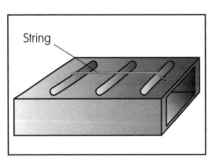

The monochord, a device used by the Pythagoreans to investigate the relationships that exist between musical pitches and mathematical ratios.

had a third support that was slid back and forth under the string. It could be placed anywhere between the two end supports.

The Pythagoreans discovered that when the third support divided the length of the string into certain whole number ratios, the sounds produced by the two string segments were harmonious or consonant. This observation indicated to them that music could be described in terms of certain numerical ratios. They identified these ratios and listed them. The ratios of the lengths of the two string segments that they identified as consonant were 1:1, 1:2, 2:3, and 3:4. The ratio 1:1, of course, is the unison: Both string segments are vibrating at the same pitch. The ratio 1:2 is what musicians now call an octave. The ratio 2:3 is the perfect fifth, and the ratio 3:4 is the perfect fourth.

The identification of these whole number ratios was profoundly important to the Pythagoreans. The Pythagoreans believed that the universe itself could be reduced to ratios of whole numbers. They speculated that the same ratios that governed the monochord governed the universe in general. They believed, for example, that Earth and the five other known planets (Mercury, Venus, Mars, Jupiter, and Saturn) as well as the Sun orbited a central fire invisible to human eyes. They believed that distances from the central fire to the planets and the Sun could also be described in terms of whole number ratios. Nor was it just nature that the Pythagoreans believed could be reduced to number. They also believed that all mathematics could be expressed via whole number arithmetic.

The Pythagoreans worshipped numbers. It was part of their beliefs that certain numbers were invested with special properties. The number 4, for example, was the number of justice and retribution. The number 1 was the number of reason. When they referred to "numbers," however, they meant *only* what we would call positive, whole numbers, that is, the numbers belonging to the sequence 1, 2, 3, . . . (Notice that the consonant tones of the monochord were produced by dividing the string into simple *whole number ratios.*) They did not recognize negative numbers, the number 0, or any type of fraction as a number. Quantities that we might describe with a fraction they would describe as a ratio between two whole numbers, and although we might not make a distinction between a ratio and a fraction, we need to recognize that they did. They only recognized ratios.

To the Pythagoreans the number 1 was the generator of all numbers—by adding 1 to itself often enough they could obtain every number (or at least every number as they understood the concept). What we would use fractions to represent, they described as ratios of sums of the number 1. A consequence of this concept of number—coupled with their mystical belief that "all is number"—is that everything in the universe can be generated from the number 1. *Everything*, in the Pythagorean view, was in the end a matter of whole number arithmetic. This idea, however, was incorrect, and their discovery that their idea of number was seriously flawed is one of the most important and far-reaching discoveries in the history of mathematics.

To understand the flaw in the Pythagorean idea of number we turn to the idea of commensurability. We say that two line segments—we call them L_1 and L_2—are commensurable, if there is a third line segment—we call it L_3—with the property that the lengths L_1 and L_2 are whole number multiples of length L_3. In this sense L_3 is a "common measure" of L_1 and L_2. For example, if segment L_1 is 2 units long and L_2 is 3 units long then we can take L_3 to be 1 unit long, and we can use L_3 to measure (evenly) the lengths of both L_1 and L_2. The idea of commensurability agrees with our intuition. It agrees with our experience. Given two line segments we can always measure them and then find a line segment whose length evenly divides both. This idea is at the heart of the Pythagorean concept of number, and that is why it came as such a shock to discover that there existed pairs of line segments that were incommensurable, that is, that there exist pairs of segments that *share no common measure!*

The discovery of incommensurability was a fatal blow to the Pythagorean idea of number; that is why they are said to have tried to hide the discovery. Happily knowledge of this remarkable fact spread rapidly. Aristotle (384–332 B.C.E.) wrote about the concept and described what is now a standard proof. Aristotle's teacher, Plato (ca. 428–347 B.C.E.), described himself as having lived as an animal lives—that is, he lived without reasoning—until he learned of the concept.

It is significant that the Greeks so readily accepted the proof of the concept of incommensurability because that acceptance shows just how early truly abstract reasoning began to dominate Greek mathematical thinking. They were willing to accept a mathematical result that violated their worldview, their everyday experience, and their sense of aesthetics. They were willing to accept the idea of incommensurability because it was a logical consequence of other, previously established, mathematical results. The Greeks often expressed their understanding of the concept by saying that the length of a diagonal of a square is incommensurable with the length of one of its sides.

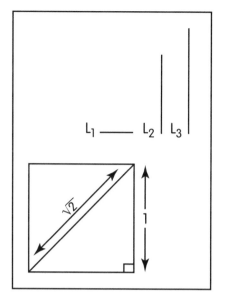

Two lengths are commensurable if they are whole number multiples of a third length. For example, segments L_2 and L_3 are commensurable because $L_2 = 2L_1$ and $L_3 = 3L_1$. Segment L_1 is called a common measure of L_2 and L_3. Not every pair of lengths is commensurable. The side of a square and its diagonal share no common measure; these segments are called incommensurable.

Incommensurability is a perfect example of the kind of result that distinguished Greek mathematical thought from the mathematical thought of all other ancient cultures. In a practical sense incommensurability is a "useless" concept. We can always find a line segment whose length is so close to the length of the diagonal of the square as to be indistinguishable from the diagonal, and we can always choose this segment with the additional property that its length and the length of a side of the square share a common measure. In a practical sense, commensurable lengths are always sufficient.

THE INCOMMENSURABILITY OF $\sqrt{2}$

The proof that the length of a diagonal of a square whose sides are 1 unit long is incommensurable with the length of a side of the square is one of the most famous proofs in the history of mathematics. The proof itself is only a few lines long. (Note that a square whose side is 1 unit long has a diagonal that is $\sqrt{2}$ units long. This is just a consequence of the Pythagorean theorem.) In modern notation the proof consists of demonstrating that there do not exist natural numbers a and b such that $\sqrt{2}$ equals a/b. The following *nonexistence proof* requires the reader to know the following two facts:

1. If a^2 is divisible by 2 then $a^2/2$ is even.
2. If b^2 (or a^2) is divisible by 2 then b (or a) is even.

We begin by assuming the opposite of what we intend to prove: We suppose that $\sqrt{2}$ *is* commensurable with 1—that is, we suppose that $\sqrt{2}$ can be written as a fraction a/b where a and b are positive whole numbers. We also assume—and this is critical—that the fraction a/b is expressed in *lowest terms*. In particular, this means that a and b cannot both be even numbers. It is okay if one is even. It is okay if neither is even, but both cannot be even or our fraction would not be in lowest terms. (Notice that if we could find integers such that $\sqrt{2} = a/b$, and if the fraction were not in lowest terms we could certainly reduce it to lowest terms. There is, therefore, no harm in assuming that it is in lowest terms from the outset.) Here is the proof:

In a theoretical sense, however, the discovery of incommensurability was an important insight into mathematics. It showed that the Pythagorean idea that everything could be expressed in terms of whole number ratios was flawed. It showed that the mathematical landscape is more complex than they originally perceived it to be. It demonstrated the importance of rigor (as opposed to intuition) in the search for mathematical truths. Greek mathematicians soon moved away from Pythagorean concepts and toward a geometric view of mathematics and the world around them. How much of this was due to the discoveries of the Pythagoreans and how much was due to the success of later generations of geometers is not clear. In any case Greek mathematics does not turn back

Suppose $a/b = \sqrt{2}$.

Now solve for b to get
$a/\sqrt{2} = b$

Finally, square both sides.
$a^2/2 = b^2$

This completes the proof. Now we have to read off what the last equation tells us. First, a^2 is evenly divisible by 2. (The quotient is b^2.) Therefore, by fact 2, a is even. Second, since $a^2/2$ is even (this follows by fact 1) b^2—which *is* $a^2/2$—is also even. Fact 2 enables us to conclude that b is even as well. Since both a and b are even our assumption that a/b is in lowest terms cannot be true. This is the contradiction that we wanted. We have proved that a and b do not exist.

This proof resonated through mathematics for more than 2,000 years. It showed that intuition is not always a good guide to truth in mathematics. It showed that the number system is considerably more complicated than it first appeared. Finally, and perhaps unfortunately, mathematicians learned from this proof to describe $\sqrt{2}$ and other similar numbers in terms of what they are *not*: $\sqrt{2}$ is not expressible as a fraction with whole numbers in the numerator and denominator. Numbers like $\sqrt{2}$ came to be called irrational numbers. A definition of irrational numbers in terms of what they *are* would have to wait until the late 19th century and the work of the German mathematician Richard Dedekind.

toward the study of algebra as a separate field of study for about 700 years.

Geometric Algebra

The attempt by the Pythagoreans to reduce mathematics to the study of whole number ratios was not successful, and Greek mathematics soon shifted away from the study of number and ratio and toward the study of geometry, the branch of mathematics that deals with points, curves, surfaces, solid figures, and their spatial relationships. The Greeks did not study geometry only as a branch of knowledge; they used it as a tool to study everything

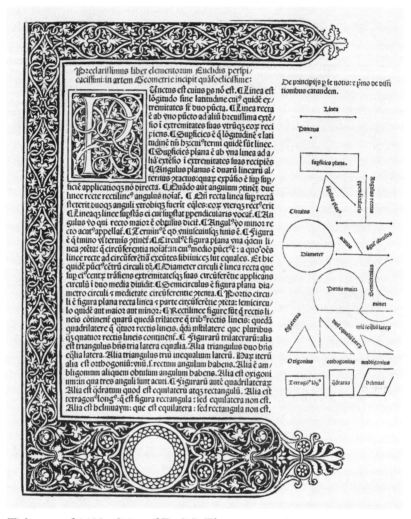

Title page of 1482 edition of Euclid's Elements. (Library of Congress, Prints and Photographs Division)

from astronomy to the law of the lever. Geometry became the language that the Greeks used to describe and understand the world about them. It should come as no surprise, then, that the Greeks also learned to use the language of geometry to express ideas that we learn to express algebraically. We call this

ALGEBRA MADE VISIBLE

Today one of the first ideas that students learn as they begin to study algebra is that "multiplication distributes over addition." This is called the distributive law and in symbols it looks like this:

$$x(y + z) = xy + xz$$

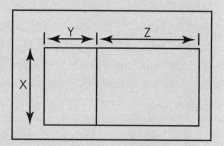

Diagram of Euclid's proof that xy + xz = x(y + z).

Though most of us eventually succeed in learning this rule, few of us could give a reason why it might be true. The very first proposition that Euclid proves in book II of the *Elements* is exactly this statement, but it is expressed in the language of geometrical algebra. More than 2,000 years ago Euclid expresses the distributive law in the following words:

> If there be two straight lines, and one of them be cut into any number of segments whatever, the rectangle contained by the two straight lines is equal to the rectangles contained by the uncut straight line and each of the segments.

(Euclid. Elements. Translated by Sir Thomas L. Heath. Great Books of the Western World, vol. 11. Chicago: Encyclopaedia Britannica, 1952.)

See the pictorial version of Euclid's statement. Notice that the illustration shows three rectangles, two smaller ones and a large one. (The large rectangle is made of the four outside line segments. The smaller rectangles lie inside the large one.) All three rectangles have the same height. We use *x* to represent the height of each of the rectangles. The rectangle on the left has length *y* and the rectangle on the right has length *z*. The length of the largest rectangle is *y* + *z*. Now we recall the formula for the area of a rectangle: Area = length × width. Finally, we can express the idea that the area of the largest rectangle equals the area of the two smaller rectangles by using the algebraic equation given. When the distributive law is expressed geometrically the reason that it is true is obvious.

geometric algebra, and it is an important part of the mathematical legacy of the ancient Greeks. Today the principal source of Greek ideas about geometric algebra is the set of books entitled *Elements* by Euclid of Alexandria, who lived in Alexandria, Egypt, in the third century B.C.E.

Little is known about Euclid. Although he lived in Alexandria, Egypt, he may have been born elsewhere. We do not know when he was born or when he died. We know that the institution where Euclid worked—it was called the Museum—was home to many of the most successful Greek mathematicians of the time. We know that many of the mathematicians who lived and worked at the school were born elsewhere. Perhaps the same can be said of Euclid.

Euclid is best remembered for having written one of the most popular textbooks of all time. Called *Elements*, it has been translated into most of the world's major languages over the last 2,000 years. In recent years it has fallen out of favor as a textbook, but many high school treatments of plane geometry are still only simplified versions of parts of Euclid's famous work. To describe the *Elements* solely as a textbook, however, is to misrepresent its impact. The type of geometry described in Euclid's textbook—now called Euclidean geometry, though it was not Euclid's invention—dominated mathematical thought for 2,000 years. We now know that there are other kinds of geometry, but as late as 200 years ago many mathematicians and philosophers insisted that Euclidean geometry was the single true geometry of the universe; if a geometry was not Euclidean, it was not "real." It was not until the 19th century that mathematicians began to realize that Euclidean geometry was simply one kind of geometry and that other, equally valid geometries exist.

The *Elements* was written in 13 brief books. Of special interest to us is the very brief book II, which lays out the foundations of geometric algebra. In book II we see how thoroughly geometric thinking pervaded all of Greek mathematics including algebra. For example, when we speak of unknowns, x, y, and z, we generally assume that these variables represent numbers. Part of learning elementary algebra involves learning the rules that enable us to manipulate these symbols as if they were numbers. Euclid's approach is quite different. In Euclid's time "variables" were not numbers. Euclid represented unknowns by line segments, and in his second book he establishes the rules that allow one to manipulate segments in the way that we would manipulate numbers. What we represent with equations, Euclid represented with pictures of triangles, rectangles, and other forms. Geometric algebra is algebra made visible.

Much of the geometry that one finds in the *Elements* is performed with a straightedge and compass. This is constructible mathematics in the sense that the truth of various mathematical statements can be demonstrated through the use of these implements. Though it would be hard to imagine simpler implements, the Greeks used these devices successfully to investigate many important mathematical ideas. As any set of techniques has, however, the use of the straightedge and compass has its limitations. Although it is not immediately apparent, certain classes of problems cannot be solved by using straightedge and compass techniques. The Greeks never discovered what kinds of limitations they imposed on themselves by their choice of these tools. As it turned out, their mathematical development was, at times, hindered by their insistence on the use of a straightedge and compass. In fact, some of the most famous mathematical problems from antiquity are famous precisely because they *cannot* be solved by using a straightedge and compass.

There are three classical geometry problems—first mentioned in the introduction of this book—that are very important in the history of algebra. Their importance in geometry is that they remained unsolved for more than 2,000 years. They were not unsolved because they were neglected. These problems attracted some of the best mathematical minds for generation after generation. Interesting mathematical ideas and techniques were discovered as individuals grappled with these problems and searched for solutions, but in the end none of these mathematicians could solve any of the three problems as originally stated, nor could they show that solutions did not exist. The problems are as follows:

Problem 1: Given an arbitrary angle, divide the angle into three equal parts, *using only a straightedge and compass.*

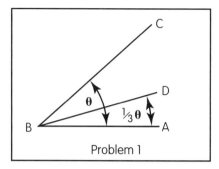

Trisecting the angle: Given angle ABC, use a straightedge and compass to construct angle ABD so that the measure of angle ABD is one-third that of the measure of angle ABC.

Problem 2: Given a circle, construct a square having the same area as the circle, *using only a straightedge and compass.*

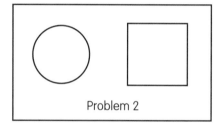

Squaring the circle: Given a circle and using only a straightedge and compass, construct a square of equal area.

Problem 3: Given a cube, find the length of the side of a new cube whose volume is twice that of the original cube. Do this *using only a straightedge and compass.*

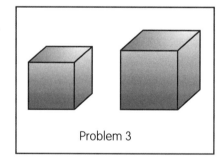

Doubling the cube: Given a cube and using only a straightedge and compass, construct a second cube that has precisely twice the volume of the original cube.

Notice that each problem has the same restriction: using only a straightedge and compass. This is critical. It is also critical to remember that the Greeks were not interested in approximate solutions to these problems. They were only interested in exact solutions. The Greeks could have easily constructed highly accurate *approximations* to a third of an angle, a squared circle, and a cube with a volume approximately twice as large as the given cube—and all with only a straightedge and compass. But approximations were not their goal. These ancient Greek geometers were searching for a method that would in theory give them the exact solution—not a good approximation to the solution—to each of the three problems.

These three problems are probably more important in the history of algebra than in the history of geometry. In algebra the search for the solutions of these problems gave birth to a new concept of what algebra is. In the 19th century, after some extraordinary breakthroughs in algebraic thought, these problems were disposed of once and for all. Nineteenth-century mathematicians discovered that the reason these problems had remained unsolved for 2,000 years was that they are unsolvable. Remember: This was proved by using algebra, not geometry. The ideas required to prove that these problems were unsolvable represented a huge step forward in the history of algebra.

The geometric algebra described by Euclid set the standard for Greek algebraic thinking for centuries. His exposition was logically rigorous, and because it was so visual it was also aesthetically appealing. But the geometric algebra found in book II of *Elements* was also too simple to be very useful. Elementary results had been obtained by sophisticated techniques. The reliance on formal, very sophisticated geometric reasoning made it difficult to extend the ideas described by Euclid. A new approach to algebra was needed.

Diophantus of Alexandria

Diophantus is often described as the father of algebra. He was, perhaps, the only one of the great Greek mathematicians to devote himself fully to the study of algebra as a discipline separate from geometry. We know little of his life. The dates of his birth and death are unknown. We do know that he lived in Alexandria, Egypt. It is generally believed that he was alive during the third century C.E., but even this is not certain; some scholars believe that he was alive during the second century C.E., and some believe that he was alive during the fourth century C.E. What are thought to be the facts of his life are usually summed up in this ancient mathematics problem:

> God granted him to be a boy for the sixth part of his life, and adding a twelfth part to this, He clothed his cheeks with down; He lit him the light of wedlock after a seventh part, and five years after his marriage He granted him a son. Alas! Late-born child; after attaining the measure of half his father's life, chill Fate took him. After consoling his grief by this science of numbers for four years he ended his life.
>
> *(Reprinted by permission of the publishers and the Trustees of Loeb Classical Library from* Greek Anthology: *Volume V, Loeb Classical Library. Volume L 86, translated by W. R. Paton, Cambridge, Mass.: Harvard University Press, 1918)*

By solving the (linear) equation that is described in the problem, we learn that Diophantus lived to be 84 years old.

Diophantus's contribution to algebra consists of two works, the more famous of which is entitled *Arithmetica*. The other is *On Polygonal Numbers*. Neither work exists in its entirety. *Arithmetica* originally consisted of 13 volumes. Six volumes were preserved in the original Greek, and in the 1970s previously unknown Arabic translations of four more volumes were discovered. Even less of *On Polygonal Numbers* has come down to us; it is known through a set of excerpts.

Arithmetica is arranged much as the *Nine Chapters* and the Mesopotamian problem texts are. Like other ancient algebralike mathematical texts, Diophantus's work is essentially a long list of problems. The exception occurs at the beginning of the first volume, in which he attempts to give an account of the foundations of algebra. This is historic because it is the first time that anyone tried to do this.

With respect to the number system that he uses, he describes rational numbers—numbers that can be represented as fractions with whole numbers in the numerator and the denominator—and negative numbers. He gives rules for working with negative numbers, and he seems comfortable enough with this system. But when solving problems, he clearly prefers solutions that are nonnegative.

Unlike the *Nine Chapters* and the other books mentioned previously, *Arithmetica* is largely devoid of nonmathematical references. It is concerned with the properties of numbers and equations, and Diophantus used no nonmathematical terminology in the expression of these ideas. There are no references to the division of corn, the height of a tree, or the area of a field. These are "pure" problems, and in that spirit he is intent on finding only exact solutions. Approximation of a solution, no matter how accurate, is not acceptable to Diophantus. In this sense *Arithmetica* is more philosophical than practical. Although Diophantus certainly knows about incommensurable (irrational) numbers, he does not consider them to be acceptable solutions to any of his equations. He searches for and accepts only rational numbers as solutions.

Another important contribution that Diophantus makes to algebra is his use of symbolism. All of the works that we have examined so far, whether written in Mesopotamia, Egypt, or China, were of a rhetorical character—that is, everything is expressed in words. This format tends to hinder progress in mathematics because it obscures the ideas and techniques involved. Diophantus introduced abbreviations and some symbols into his work. We call this mixture of abbreviations, words, and a few symbols syncopated algebra. Diophantus's syncopated algebra lacks the compact form of contemporary algebraic equations. It is not especially easy to read, but he went further toward developing a specialized system of symbols than any of his predecessors.

The problems that Diophantus studied often had multiple solutions. The existence of multiple solutions for a single problem would immediately catch the eye of any contemporary mathematician, but Diophantus usually seems not to care. If he can find even one solution he seems content. Did he know that in some cases other solutions exist? It is not always clear. On the other hand, Diophantus is very interested in *how* a solution is found, and he sometimes describes more than one method for solving the same problem. It is clear that algorithms are a primary focus for him.

It is tempting to see in Diophantus's exhausting list of problems and solutions the search for a rigorous theory of algebraic equations that is analogous to the highly developed system of geometry that the Greeks had developed centuries earlier. If that was his goal, he did not achieve it. There is no overarching concept to Diophantus's algebra. It is, instead, a collection of adroitly chosen problems, whose solutions more often than not depend on a clever trick rather than a deeper theoretical understanding. Nevertheless, there is no work that survives from antiquity in any culture that rivals Diophantus's *Arithmetica* as an algebraic text. Though he does not introduce unity to his subject, he greatly raises the level of abstraction. In Diophantus's work we find algebra stripped of all nonmathematical references, with the equations themselves displayed as objects that deserve study in their own right. Perhaps more importantly, *Arithmetica* served as a source of insight and inspiration for generations of Islamic and European mathematicians. And about 1,500 years after Diophantus wrote *Arithmetica*, his work inspired the French mathematician Pierre de Fermat to attempt to generalize one of the problems that he found in *Arithmetica* about representing one square as the sum of two squares. This gave rise to what is now called Fermat's last theorem, one of the most famous of all mathematical problems and one that was not solved until late in the 20th century.

Greek algebra—whether it is like that found in *Elements* or in *Arithmetica*—is characterized by a higher level of abstraction than that found in other ancient mathematically sophisticated cultures. Both the choice of problems and method of presentation were unique among the cultures of antiquity, and the Greek influence on future generations of Arab and European mathematicians was profound. New approaches to algebra that were eventually developed elsewhere, however, would prove to be equally important.

3

ALGEBRA FROM INDIA TO NORTHERN AFRICA

The tradition of Greek mathematical research ended in the third century C.E. with the death of Hypatia (ca. 370–415) in Alexandria. Hypatia was a prominent scholar and mathematician. She wrote commentaries on the works of Diophantus, Apollonius, and Ptolemy, but all of her work has been lost. We know of her through the works and letters of other scholars of the time. Hypatia was murdered in a religious dispute. Shortly thereafter many of the

The death of Hypatia marked the end of the Greek mathematical tradition.
(ARPL/Topham/The Image Works)

scholars in Alexandria left, and mathematical research at Alexandria, the last of the great Greek centers of learning, ended.

Mathematics, however, continued to develop in new ways and in new locations. In the Western Hemisphere the Mayan civilization was developing a unique and advanced form of mathematics. We know of some of their accomplishments, but most of their work was destroyed by Spanish conquerors in the 16th century. Another new and important center of mathematical research developed on the Indian subcontinent, but before examining the accomplishments of these mathematicians it is important to say a few words about terminology.

The mathematical tradition that developed on the Indian subcontinent during this time is sometimes called Indian mathematics. It was not created entirely in what is now India. Some of it arose in what is now Pakistan, and, in any case, India was not united under a central government during the period of interest to us. There was no India in the modern sense. There are some histories of "Indian" mathematics that use the term *Hindu mathematics*, but not all of the mathematicians who contributed to the development of this mathematical tradition were themselves Hindu. There are no other terms in general use. We use the terms *Indian mathematics* and *Hindu mathematics* interchangeably because they are the two common names for this mathematical tradition, but neither term is entirely satisfactory. We look forward to the time when better, more descriptive terminology is developed to describe the accomplishments of this creative and heterogeneous people.

There are widely varying claims made about the history of Indian mathematics. Some scholars think that a sophisticated Hindu mathematical tradition goes back several thousand years, but the evidence for this claim is indirect. Very few records from the more remote periods of Indian history have survived. Some of the earliest records of Indian mathematical accomplishments are the *Sulvasutras*, a collection of results in geometry and geometric algebra. The dating of these works is also a matter of dispute. Some scholars believe that they date to the time of Pythagoras, but others claim they were written several centuries after Pythagoras's death. Mathematically the *Sulvasutras* are, in any case, not especially sophisticated when compared with the Hindu works that are of most interest to us. In fact, it is their simplicity that is the best indicator that they preceded the works for which we do have reliable dates.

Despite their simplicity, the *Sulvasutras* contain many qualities that are characteristic of much of the Indian mathematical tradition. It is important to review these special characteristics, because Indian mathematics is quite distinct from that of the other mathematically sophisticated cultures that preceded it. Moreover, even when there is overlap between the mathematics of India and that of ancient Greece or Mesopotamia, it is clear that Indian mathematicians perceived mathematics differently. The mathematics of the Indians is often compared unfavorably to Greek mathematics, but such comparisons are not especially helpful. Hindu mathematics is better appreciated on its own terms. Mathematics occupied a different place in the culture of the Hindus than it did in the culture of the Greeks.

One characteristic of Hindu mathematics is that almost all of it—problems, rules, and definitions—is written in verse. This is true of the *Sulvasutras* and virtually all later works as well. Another characteristic property that we find in the *Sulvasutras* as well as later Hindu mathematics is that there are no proofs that the rules that one finds in the texts are correct. Ancient Indian texts contain almost no mathematical rigor, as we understand the term today. The rules that one finds in these texts were sometimes illustrated with one or more examples. The examples were sometimes followed with challenges directed to the reader, but there was little in the way of motivation or justification for the rules themselves. This was not simply a matter of presentation. The mathematicians who created this highly imaginative approach to mathematics must have had only a minimal interest in proving that the results they obtained were correct, because mistakes in the texts themselves often were unnoticed. Many of the best Hindu works contain a number of significant errors, but these works also contain important discoveries, some of which have had a profound effect on the entire history of mathematics.

Another important difference between Indian mathematics and the mathematics of other cultures with advanced mathematical traditions is that other cultures perceived mathematics as a separate field of study. In the Indian cultural tradition, mathematics was not usually treated as an independent branch of knowledge. There are very few ancient Sanskrit texts devoted solely to mathematics. Instead mathematical knowledge was usually conveyed in isolated chapters in larger works about astronomy. Astronomy and religion were very much intertwined in the classical culture of the Indian subcontinent. To many of the most important Hindu mathematicians, mathematics was a tool for better understanding the motions and relative locations of objects in the night sky. It was not a separate academic discipline.

Brahmagupta and the New Algebra

The astronomer and mathematician Brahmagupta (ca. 598–ca. 670) was one of the most important of all Indian mathematicians. Not much is known about his life. It is known that he lived in Ujjain, a town located in what is now central India. In Brahmagupta's time Ujjain was home to an important astronomical observatory, and Brahmagupta was head of the observatory. Brahmagupta's major work is a book on astronomy, *Brahma-sphuta-siddhānta* (The opening of the universe). Written entirely in verse, Brahmagupta's masterpiece is 25 chapters long. Most of the book contains information about astronomical phenomena: the prediction of eclipses, the determination of the positions of the planets, the phases of the Moon, and so on. Just two of the chapters are about mathematics, but those two chapters contain a great deal of important algebra.

Brahmagupta's work, like that of other Hindu mathematicians, contains plenty of rules. Most are stated without proof; nor does he provide information about how he arrived at these rules or why he believes them to be true. Many rules are, however, followed by problems to illustrate how the rules can be applied. Here, for example, is Brahmagupta's "rule of inverse operation":

The ancient astronomical observatory at Ujjain. This site has many exotic pieces of "celestial architecture" used in the study of astronomy. (Dinodia/The Image Works)

Multiplier must be made divisor; and divisor, multiplier; positive, negative and negative, positive; root [is to be put] for square; and square, for root; and first as converse for last.

> *(Brahmagupta and Bhaskara.* Algebra with Arithmetic and Mensuration. *Translated by Henry Colebrook. London: John Murray, 1819)*

By modern standards this is a fairly terse explanation, but by the standards of the day it was comparatively easy reading. To understand why, it helps to know that Brahmagupta, like many Indian mathematicians, probably grew up reading just this type of explanation. Indian astronomical and mathematical knowledge was generally passed from one generation to the next within the same family. Each generation studied astronomy, mathematics, and astrology and contributed to the family library. Brahmagupta's father, for example, was a well-known astrologer. Mathematical writing and astronomical writing were important parts of Brahmagupta's family tradition. He would have been accustomed to this kind of verse, but he advanced well beyond what he inherited from his forebears.

One of the most important characteristics of Brahmagupta's work is his style of algebraic notation. It is, like that of Diophantus, syncopated algebra. Syncopated algebra uses specialized symbols and abbreviations of words to convey the ideas involved. For instance, Brahmagupta used a dot above a number to indicate a negative number. When formulating an equation containing one or more unknowns, Brahmagupta called each unknown a different color. His use of colors is completely analogous to the way that we are taught to use the letters x, y, and z to represent variables when we first learn algebra. To simplify his notation he preferred to use an abbreviated form of each color word. One section of his book is even called Equations of Several Colors.

One consequence of his notation is that his mathematical prose is fairly abstract, and this characteristic is important for two reasons. First, a condensed, abstract algebraic notation often makes mathematical ideas more transparent and easy to express. Second, good algebraic notation makes adopting a very general and inclusive approach to problem solving easier, and generality is just what Brahmagupta achieved.

To appreciate the generality of Brahmagupta's approach we need only compare it with that of Diophantus. Brahmagupta considered the equation that we would write as $ax + by = c$, where a, b, and c are integers (whole numbers), called coefficients, that could be positive, negative, or zero. The letters x and y denote the *variables* that are meant to represent whole number solutions to the equation. Brahmagupta's goal was to locate whole numbers that, when substituted for x and y, made the equation a true statement about numbers.

Brahmagupta's very broad understanding of what a, b, and c represent stands in sharp contrast with the work of Diophantus. Diophantus preferred to consider only equations in which the coefficients are positive. This required Diophantus to break Brahmagupta's single equation into several special cases. If, for example, b was less than 0 in the preceding equation, Diophantus would add $-b$ to both sides of the equation to obtain $ax = -by + c$. (If b is negative, $-b$ is positive.) This equation, with the b transposed to the other side, was a distinct case to Diophantus, but

Brahmagupta, because he did not distinguish between positive and negative coefficients, had to consider only the single equation $ax + by = c$. This allowed him to achieve a more general, more modern, and more powerful approach to the solution of algebraic equations. Furthermore, he accepted negative numbers as solutions, a concept with which his Greek predecessors had difficulty.

This highly abstract approach to the solution of algebraic equations is also characteristic of Brahmagupta's work with second-degree algebraic equations. When he solved second-degree algebraic equations, also called quadratic equations, he seemed to see all quadratic equations as instances of the single model equation $ax^2 + bx + c = 0$, where the coefficients a, b, and c could represent negative as well as nonnegative numbers. Brahmagupta was willing to accept negative solutions here as well. He also accepted rational and irrational numbers as solutions. (A *rational number* can be represented as the quotient of two whole numbers. An *irrational number* is a number that cannot be represented as the quotient of two whole numbers.) This willingness to expand the number system to fit the problem, rather than to restrict the problem to fit the number system, is characteristic of much of the best Indian mathematics.

Finally, Brahmagupta, as Diophantus was, was interested in indeterminate equations. (An *indeterminate equation* is a single equation, or a system of equations, with many solutions.) When considering these types of problems he attempted to find all possible solutions subject to certain restrictions.

Brahmagupta's work is algorithmic in nature. To Brahmagupta learning new math meant learning new techniques to solve equations. Today many of us think of mathematics as the search for solutions to difficult word problems, but mathematics has always been about more than finding the right solutions. The Greeks, for example, were often more concerned with discovering new properties of geometric figures than they were with performing difficult calculations. Brahmagupta was familiar with other approaches to mathematics, but he was motivated by problems that involved difficult calculations. He wanted to find calculating techniques that yielded answers, and he had a very broad idea of what constituted an answer. The *Brahma-sphuta-siddhānta* was quickly recognized by Brahmagupta's contemporaries as an important and imaginative work. It inspired numerous commentaries by many generations of mathematicians.

Mahavira

The mathematician Mahavira (ca. 800–ca. 870), also known as Mahaviracharya, was one of those inspired by *Brahma-sphuta-siddhānta* (Compendium of the essence of mathematics) Mahavira lived in southern India. He was an unusual figure in the history of Hindu mathematics. He was not, for example, a Hindu. He was a member of the Jain religion. (Jainism is a small but culturally important religious sect in present-day India.) He was not an astronomer. His book, called *Ganita Sara Samgraha*, is the first book in the Indian mathematical tradition that confines its attention to pure mathematics. It is sometimes described as a commentary on Brahmagupta's work, but it is more than that. Mahavira's book is an ambitious attempt to summarize, improve upon, and teach Indian mathematical knowledge as he understood it. Mahavira's book was very successful. It was widely circulated and used by students for several centuries.

There are traditional aspects of Mahavira's book. As Brahmagupta's great work, *Brahma-sphuta-siddhānta*, is, Mahavira's book is written in verse and consists of rules and examples. The rules are stated without proof. Coupled with his very traditional presentation is a very modern approach to arithmetic. It is presented in a way that is similar to the way arithmetic is taught today.

In addition to his presentation of arithmetic, Mahavira demonstrated considerable skill manipulating the Hindu system of numeration: He constructed math problems whose answers read the same forward and backward. For example: $14287143 \times 7 = 100010001$. (Notice that the answer to the multiplication problem is a sort of numerical palindrome.) He was also interested in algebraic identities. (An identity is a mathematical statement that is true for all numbers.) An example of one of the identities that Mahavira discovered is $a^3 = a(a + b)(a - b) + b^2 (a - b) + b^3$. These kinds of identities sometimes facilitate calculation. They also demonstrate how various algebraic quantities relate one to another.

Word problems were also important to Mahavira. He included numerous carefully crafted problems in *Ganita Sara Samgraha*. Some of the problems are elementary, but some require a fair bit of algebra to solve.

Mahavira exercises his algebraic insights on two other classes of problems. In one section of the book he studies combinatorics. Combinatorics, which generally requires a fairly extensive knowledge of algebra, deals with the way different combinations of objects can be chosen from a fixed set. It is the kind of knowledge that is now widely used in the study of probability. He shows, for example, that the number of ways r objects can be chosen from a set containing n objects is

$$\frac{n\ (n-1)\ (n-2) \ldots (n-r+1)}{r\ (r-1)\ (r-2) \ldots 2 \cdot 1}$$

where we have written his result in modern notation. This is an important formula that is widely used today.

The second class of algebra problems is geometric in origin. In Mahavira's hands even the geometry problems—and there are a number of them—are just another source of algebraic equations. For example, he attempts to find the dimensions of two triangles with the following properties: (1) the areas of the triangles are equal and (2) the perimeter of one is twice that of the other. This problem leads to some fairly sophisticated algebra. This is a nice example of an indeterminate problem—it has many solutions.

More generally, there are several points worth noting about Mahavira's work. First, like Brahmagupta's work, Mahavira's writings are a highly syncopated approach to algebra. (Algebra is called syncopated when it is expressed in a combination of words, abbreviations, and a few specialized symbols.) Second, the emphasis in much of the book is on developing the techniques necessary to solve algebraic problems. It is a tour de force approach to solving various types of equations, but he provides no broader context into which we can place his results. Each problem stands on its own with no consideration given to a broader theory of equations. Third, there are no proofs or carefully developed logical arguments. He shows the reader results that he believes are important, but he often does not show the reader why he considers the results correct. His ideas are creative, but because of his lack of emphasis on mathematical proofs when he makes an error, even a glaring error, he sometimes fails to catch it. For example, when he tries to compute the area of an ellipse, he gets it wrong. Given the level of mathematics in Mahavira's time, this was admittedly a difficult problem. Perhaps he could not have solved the problem by using the mathematics available at the time, but with a more rigorous approach to the problem he might have been able to discover what the answer is *not*.

Bhaskara and the End of an Era

The discoveries of Brahmagupta, Mahavira, and many other mathematicians in the Indian tradition probably found their highest expression in the work of the mathematician and astronomer Bhaskara (1114–ca. 1185). Bhaskara, also known as Bhaskaracharya and Bhaskara II, was the second prominent Indian mathematician of that name. (We will have no reason to refer to the first.) Bhaskara was born in southern India, in the city of Bijapur in the same general region in which Mahavira was born. Unlike Mahavira, but like Brahmagupta, Bhaskara was an astronomer. He eventually moved to Ujjain, where he became head of the astronomical observatory there. It was the same observatory that Brahmagupta had directed several centuries earlier.

Bhaskara's main work, *Siddhānta Siromani* (Head jewel of accuracy), is a book about astronomy and mathematics. It is divided into four sections, covering arithmetic, algebra, the celestial sphere, and various planetary calculations. Like the other texts we have considered, the *Siddhānta Siromani* is written in verse, although Bhaskara also provides an additional section written in prose that explains some of the mathematics found in the main body of the work. Sanskrit scholars have praised Bhaskara's work both for the quality of its poetry and for its mathematical content. At one point in *Siddhānta Siromani* Bhaskara claims to summarize the work of Brahmagupta and two other mathematicians. We can compare his work with that of Brahmagupta to see what parts of Brahmagupta's work he used, but the work of the other two mathematicians has been lost. Furthermore, although Bhaskara's work in combinatorics seems to owe much to Mahavira's book, he does not mention Mahavira in his acknowledgment. Bhaskara's book does, however, go beyond Mahavira's. For these reasons it is not clear whether Bhaskara was mathematically far above his contemporaries or whether his work simply reflected a very high level of mathematical achievement in the city of Ujjain at the time that it was written.

Bhaskara uses a highly syncopated algebraic notation. He solves a variety of determinate and indeterminate equations, and he is open to the possibility that the solutions to the equations that he solves may be negative as well as positive, and irrational as well as rational. He looks at very general first- and second-degree algebraic equations and seems comfortable with coefficients that are negative as well as positive. He even suggests special rules for doing arithmetic with certain irrational numbers. In many ways the work that Bhaskara did on second-degree algebraic equations is identical to work that high school students do today. Although this point may sound elementary, it was not. Mathematicians took millennia to extend their idea of number, their idea of solution, and their computational techniques to solve these types of equations. Furthermore, there are many aspects of Bhaskara's work with algebraic equations that were not surpassed anywhere in the world for several centuries.

The Leelavati and the Bijaganita, the two sections of his work that are mathematical in nature, are full of word problems to challenge the reader. He writes about swans, bees, and monkeys. Bhaskara worked hard to engage the reader with well-written, interesting exercises. One problem describes a bamboo plant, 32 cubits long, growing out of level ground. The wind springs up and breaks the plant. The top of the plant falls over, and the tip of the plant just touches the ground at a distance of 16 cubits from the

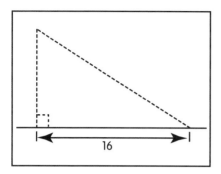

A problem by Bhaskara: Before the plant broke it was 32 cubits tall. After it broke the distance from the top of the plant (now on the ground) to the base is 16 cubits. At what height did the break occur?

base of the stalk. Bhaskara challenges the reader to compute the distance above the ground at which the stalk snapped. Interestingly, this same problem can also be found in ancient Chinese mathematical literature. (The answer is that the stalk snapped 12 cubits above the ground.)

Bhaskara's interest in the technical issues involved in solving particular equations allowed him to make great progress in special cases, and his work with the quadratic equation was very general, but in most cases, the progress that Bhaskara achieves is incremental progress. He absorbs the work of his predecessors and extends it. Most of what he did, from his use of verse, to his indifference to the concept of proof, to his choice of problems, and to his preference for algebraic as opposed to geometric methods, is reminiscent of the work of Indian mathematicians who preceded him. What distinguishes his work is that it is generally more advanced than that of his predecessors. He expresses his ideas with greater clarity. His approach is more general, that is, more abstract, and so he sees more deeply into each problem. Finally his work is more complete. The *Siddhānta Siromani* influenced many generations of mathematicians. It was a major achievement. It is sometimes described as the most important mathematical text to emerge from the classical Indian mathematical tradition.

Islamic Mathematics

The origins of Indian mathematics, Egyptian mathematics, and Mesopotamian mathematics, to name three prominent examples, lie thousands of years in the past. Records that might help us

POETRY AND ALGEBRA

It is an oft-repeated remark that in a poem, the poetry is the part that is lost in translation. If this is true for translations of verse between modern languages, the "loss of poetry" must be even more pronounced when ancient Sanskrit verse is translated to modern English. Nevertheless, skillful translations are the only means that most of us have of appreciating the poetry in which the mathematicians of ancient India expressed themselves. Here are two word problems, originally composed in verse in Sanskrit, by Bhaskara:

1.) One pair out of a flock of geese remained sporting in the water, and saw seven times the half of the square-root of the flock proceeding to the shore tired of the diversion. Tell me, dear girl, the number of the flock.

The algebraic equation to be solved is $(7/2)\sqrt{x} = x - 2$.
The solutions to the equation are $x = 16$ and $x = 1/4$.
The only reasonable solution to the word problem is $x = 16$.

2.) Out of a heap of pure lotus flowers, a third part, a fifth and a sixth, were offered respectively to the gods Siva, Vishńu and the Sun; and a quarter was presented to Bhaváníi. The remaining six lotuses were given to the venerable preceptor. Tell quickly the whole number of flowers. (ibid.)

The algebraic equation to be solved is

$$x - \left(\frac{1}{3} + \frac{1}{5} + \frac{1}{6} + \frac{1}{4} \right) x = 6$$

The solution to the mathematical equation is $x = 120$.

(Brahmagupta and Bhaskara. Algebra with Arithmetic and Mensuration. *Translated by Henry Colebrook. London: John Murray, 1819)*

understand how mathematics arose in these cultures are sometimes too sparse to provide much insight. This is not the case with Islamic mathematics.

Historically Islamic culture begins with the life of Muhammad (570–632). Historical records are reasonably good. We can refer to

The Great Mosque at Samarra was built about 60 miles from Baghdad, al-Khwārizmī's home, near the end of the mathematician's life. (Josef Polleross/The Image Works)

documents by Islamic historians as well as their non-Muslim neighbors. We know quite a bit about how mathematics in general, and algebra in particular, arose in the Islamic East, and this is important, because within 200 years of the death of the Prophet Muhammad great centers of learning had been established. A new and important mathematical tradition arose. This new tradition had a profound influence on the history of mathematics: Algebra was the great contribution of Islamic mathematicians. But the term *Islamic mathematics* must be used with care.

Islamic mathematics is the term traditionally given to the mathematics that arose in the area where Islam was the dominant religion, but just as the term *Hindu mathematics* is not entirely satisfactory, neither is *Islamic mathematics* quite the right term. Although Islam was the dominant religion in the region around Baghdad in what is now Iraq when algebraic research flourished, Jews and Christians also lived in the area. For the most part, they were free to practice their religions unmolested. Although most of the prominent mathematical scholars of the time had the Islamic faith, there was also room for others at even the most prominent institutions of higher learning. A number of Christian scholars, for example, helped to translate the ancient Greek mathematical texts that were stored at the House of Wisdom in Baghdad, one of the great centers of learning at the time. There was a notable 10th-century Jewish mathematician who published "Islamic" mathematics named Abu 'Otman Sahl ibn Bishr, ibn Habib ibn Hani; and one of the most prominent mathematicians of his day, Ali-sabi Thabit ibn Qurra al-Harrani, was a Sabean, a member of a sect that traced its roots to a religion of the ancient Mesopotamians. Despite this diversity, *Islamic mathematics* is the name often given to this mathematics because the Islamic faith had a strong cultural as well as religious impact.

Sometimes this mathematics is called Arabic, but not all the mathematicians involved were Arabic, either. Of the two choices, Arabic or Islamic mathematics, Islamic mathematics seems the more accurate description. Islam affected everything from governmental institutions to architectural practices. So we adopt the common practice of calling our subject Islamic mathematics, even though math, in the end, has no religious affiliation, because the Islamic society of the time was tolerant and heterogeneous, and the work of Islamic mathematicians has found a secure place in the mathematics practiced around the world today.

The history of Islamic mathematics begins in earnest with the life of al-Ma'mūn (786–833). Although al-Ma'mūn is an important figure in the history of algebra, he was no mathematician. He is best remembered for his accomplishments as a political leader. He was the son of the caliph Hārūn ar-Rashīd. (The caliphs, as were the kings of the time, were absolute rulers of their nations.) Ar-Rashīd had another son, al-Ma'mūn's half-brother, named al-Amīn. After the father's death the two brothers, al-Ma'mūn and al-Amīn, led their respective factions in a brutal four-year civil war over succession rights to the caliphate. In the end al-Amīn lost both the war and his life.

As caliph al-Ma'mūn proved to be a creative, if ruthless, political leader. He worked hard, though not entirely successfully, to heal the division that existed between the Shī'ite and Sunnite sects of

Islam. In Baghdad he established the House of Wisdom, an important academic institution where Greek texts in mathematics, science, and philosophy were translated and disseminated. When these works could not be obtained within the caliphate, he obtained them from the libraries of Byzantium, a sometimes-hostile power. He established astronomical observatories, and he encouraged scholars to make their own original contributions. His work bore fruit. A new approach to algebra developed in Baghdad at this time.

Al-Khwārizmī and a New Concept of Algebra

A number of mathematicians responded to al-Ma'mūn's words of encouragement and contributed to the development of a new concept of algebra. Mathematically speaking, it was a very creative time. One of the first and most talented mathematicians was named Mohammed ibn-Mūsā al-Khwārizmī (ca. 780–ca. 850). Al-Khwārizmī described what happened in these words:

> [al-Ma'mūn] has encouraged me to compose a short work on Calculating by (the rules of) Completion and Reduction, confining it to what is easiest and most useful in arithmetic.
>
> *(Al-Khwārizmī, Mohammed ibn-Mūsā.* Robert of Chester's Latin Translation of the Algebra of al-Khwārizmī. *Translated by Karpinski, Louis C. New York: The Macmillan Company, 1915)*

Al-Khwārizmī's *approach* to algebra was new and significant, but many of the results that he obtained were not. Nor was he the only mathematician of his time to use the new approach. In recent historical times scholars have discovered the work of another Islamic mathematician, Abd-al-Hamid ibn-Turk, who wrote a book about algebra that was similar to al-Khwārizmī's. This second text was written at about the same time that al-Khwārizmī's work was published. The existence of Abd-al-Hamid's book indicates that some of the mathematical ideas described by al-Khwārizmī may not have originated with him. In that sense, al-Khwārizmī may, as Euclid was, have been more of a skilled expositor than an innovator. There is not enough information to know for sure. Nevertheless al-Khwārizmī's book had the greatest long-term influence. Even the author's name became part of the English language. Al-Khwārizmī's name was mispronounced often enough in Europe to take on the form *algorismi*, and this word was later shortened to the words *algorithm*, a specialized method for solving mathematical problems, and *algorism*, the so-called Arabic system of numerals. Furthermore, the first word in the title of one of al-Khwārizmī's books, *Hisāb al-jabr wa'l muqābala*, eventually found its way into English as the word *algebra*.

Al-Khwārizmī's book *Hisāb al-jabr wa'l muqābala* has little in common with those of Brahmagupta and Diophantus. For one thing, the problems that he solves tend to be easier, because they are for the most part less advanced. Second, he avoids solutions that involve 0 or negative numbers. He avoids problems in indeterminate analysis—that is, problems for which many solutions exist—and he writes without any specialized algebraic notation. Not only does he avoid the use of letters or abbreviations for variables, he sometimes even avoids using numerals to represent numbers. He often prefers to write out the numbers in longhand. Even the motivation for Al-Khwārizmī's book was different from that of his predecessors. Diophantus seems to have had no motivation other than an interest in mathematics. Brahmagupta's motivation stemmed from his interest in mathematics and astronomy. But al-Khwārizmī wrote that al-Ma'mūn had encouraged him to develop a mathematics that would be of use in solving practical problems such as the "digging of canals" and the "division of estates."

Much of the first half of al-Khwārizmī's book *Hisāb al-jabr* is concerned with the solution of second-degree algebraic equations, but his method is not nearly as general as Brahmagupta's. Unlike Brahmagupta, he does not perceive all quadratic equations as instances of a single general type. Instead, what we would call "the" quadratic equation he perceived as a large number of separate cases. For example, he considers quadratic equations, such as $x^2 = 5x$, and he identifies the number 5 as a solution. (We would also recognize $x = 0$ as a solution, but al-Khwārizmī does not acknowledge 0 as a legitimate solution.) Because he uses rhetorical algebra, that is, an algebra devoid of specialized, algebraic symbols, his description of the equation $x^2 = 5x$ and its solution take some getting used to:

A square is equal to 5 roots. The root of the square then is 5, and 25 forms its square which, of course, equals five of its roots.

(*Al-Khwārizmī, Mohammed ibn-Mūsā.* Robert of Chester's Latin Translation of the Algebra of al-Khwārizmī. *Translated by Karpinski, Louis C. New York: The Macmillan Company, 1915*)

He plods his way from one special case to the next, and in this there is nothing new. At first it seems as if al-Khwārizmī, as his predecessor Brahmagupta and his far-away contemporary Mahavira did, sees algebra simply as a collection of problem-solving techniques. But this is not so. After establishing these results he shifts focus; it is this shift in focus that is so important to the history of algebra. After solving a number of elementary problems, he returns to the problems that he just solved and *proves* the correctness of his approach. In the field of algebra this is both new and very important.

Al-Khwārizmī's tool of choice for his proofs is geometry, but he is not interested in geometry as a branch of thought in the way that the ancient Greeks were. He is not interested in *studying* geometry; he wants to use it to provide a proof that his algebraic reasoning was without flaws. Recall that it was the lack of proofs in Hindu algebra that made it so difficult for those mathematicians to separate the true from the false. Al-Khwārizmī, by contrast, wanted to build his algebra on a solid logical foundation, and he was fortunate to have a ready-made model of deductive reasoning on hand: the classics of Greek geometry.

The geometry of the Greeks would certainly have been familiar to al-Khwārizmī. Throughout his life the translators associated with the House of Wisdom were busy translating ancient Greek works into Arabic, and there was no better example of careful mathematical reasoning available anywhere in the world at this time than in the works of the Greeks. Their works are filled with rigorous proofs. Al-Khwārizmī had the concept for a rigorous algebra and a model of mathematical rigor available. It was his great insight to combine the two into something new.

Al-Khwārizmī's interest in developing procedures for computing with square roots also bears mentioning. He begins with the very simplest examples, among them the problem of multiplying the square root of 9 by the number 2. Here is how he describes the procedure:

> Take the root of nine to be multiplied. If you wish to double the root of nine you proceed as follows: 2 by 2 gives 4, which you multiply by 9, giving 36. Take the root of this, i.e. 6, which is

A PROBLEM AND A SOLUTION

The following is an elementary problem that was posed and solved by al-Khwārizmī in his algebra. It is a nice example of rhetorical algebra, that is, algebra expressed entirely in words and without the use of specialized algebraic symbols.

If you are told, "ten for six, how much for four?" then *ten* is the measure; *six* is the price; the expression *how much* implies the unknown number of the quantity; and *four* is the number of the sum. The number of the measure, which is *ten,* is inversely proportionate to the number of the sum, namely, *four.* Multiply, therefore, ten by four, that is to say, the two known proportionate numbers by each other; the product is forty. Divide this by the other known number, which is that of the price, namely, six. The quotient is six and two-thirds; it is the unknown number, implied in the words of the question *how much?* it is the quantity, and inversely proportionate to the six, which is the price.

(*Al-Khwārizmī, Mohammed ibn-Mūsā*. Robert of Chester's Latin Translation of the Algebra of al-Khwārizmī. *Translated by Louis C. Karpinski, New York: The Macmillan Company, 1915*)

In our notation al-Khwārizmī solved the problem that we would express as $10/6 = x/4$.

found to be two roots of nine, i.e. the double of three. For three, the root of nine, added to itself gives 6.

(*Al-Khwārizmī, Mohammed ibn-Mūsā.* Robert of Chester's Latin Translation of the Algebra of al-Khwārizmī. *Translated by Karpinski, Louis C. New York: The Macmillan Company, 1915*)

In our notation we express this idea as $2\sqrt{9} = \sqrt{4 \cdot 9} = \sqrt{36} = 6$, which again emphasizes the importance and utility of our modern system of notation. He extends this simple numerical example into several more general algebraic formulas. For example, we would express one of his rhetorical equations as follows: $3\sqrt{x} = \sqrt{9x}$.

It is not clear why al-Khwārizmī avoided the use of any sort of algebraic symbolism. Without any specialized algebraic notation his work is not easy to read despite the fact that he is clearly a skilled expositor. Al-Khwārizmī's work had an important influence on the many generations of mathematicians living in the Near East, Northern Africa, and Europe. On the positive side, his concept of incorporating geometric reasoning to buttress his algebraic arguments was widely emulated. On the negative side, his highly rhetorical approach would prove a barrier to rapid progress. What is most important is that Al-Khwārizmī's work established a logical foundation for the subject he loved. His work set the standard for rigor in algebra for centuries.

Omar Khayyám, Islamic Algebra at Its Best

The astronomer, poet, mathematician, and philosopher Omar Khayyám (ca. 1050–1123) was perhaps the most important of all Islamic mathematicians after al-Khwārizmī. Omar was born in Neyshābūr (Nishāpūr) in what is now northeastern Iran. He also died in Neyshābūr, and between his birth and death he traveled a great deal. Political turbulence characterized Omar's times, and moving from place to place was sometimes a matter of necessity.

Omar was educated in Neyshābūr, where he studied mathematics and philosophy. As a young man he moved about 500 miles (800 km) to Samarqand, which at the time was a major city, located in what is now Uzbekistan. It was in Samarqand that he became well known as a mathematician. Later he accepted an invitation to work as an astronomer and director of the observatory at the city of Esfahan, which is located in central Iran. He remained there for about 18 years, until the political situation became unstable and dangerous. Funding for the observatory was withdrawn, and Omar moved to the city of Merv, now Mary, in present-day Turkmenistan. During much of his life Omar was treated with suspicion by many of his contemporaries for his freethinking and unorthodox ideas. He wrote angrily about the difficulty of doing scholarly work in the environments in which he found himself, but in retrospect he seems to have done well despite the difficulties.

Omar described algebra, a subject to which he devoted much of his life, in this way:

> By the help of God and with His precious assistance, I say that Algebra is a scientific art. The objects with which it deals are absolute numbers and measurable quantities which, though themselves unknown, are related to "things" which are known, whereby the determination of the unknown quantities is possible. Such a thing is either a quantity or a unique relation, which is only determined by careful examination. What one searches for in the algebraic art are the relations which lead from the known to the unknown, to discover which is the object of Algebra as stated above. The perfection of this art consists in knowledge of the scientific method by which one determined numerical and geometric quantities.
>
> *(Kasir, Daoud S. The Algebra of Omar Khayyám. New York: Columbia University Press, 1931. Used with permission)*

This is a good definition for certain kinds of algebra even today, almost a thousand years later. The care with which the ideas in the definition are expressed indicates that the author was a skilled writer in addition to being a skilled mathematician, but he is generally remembered as either one or the other. In the West, Omar Khayyám is best remembered as the author of *The Rubáiyát of Omar Khayyám*, a collection of poems. This collection of poems was organized, translated into English, and published in the 19th

No.	Month	Length
1	Farvardin	31
2	Ordibehesht	31
3	Khordad	31
4	Tir	31
5	Mordad	31
6	Shahrivar	31
7	Mehr	30
8	Aban	30
9	Azar	30
10	Dey	30
11	Bahman	30
12	Esfand	29 or 30

A small group of scientists, of which Omar Khayyám was the most prominent member, devised the Jalali calendar. With some modest modifications this has become today's Persian calendar (pictured above).

century. It has been in print ever since and has now been translated into all the major languages of the world. The *Rubáiyát* is a beautiful work, but Omar's skill as a poet was not widely recognized in his own time, nor is it the trait for which he is best remembered in Islamic countries today.

Omar's contemporaries knew him as a man of extraordinarily broad interests. Astronomy, medicine, law, history, philosophy, and mathematics were areas in which he distinguished himself. He made especially important contributions to mathematics and to the revision of the calendar. His revision of the calendar earned him a certain amount of fame because the calendar in use at the time was inaccurate in the sense that the calendar year and the astronomical year were of different lengths. As a consequence over time the seasons shifted to different parts of the calendar year. This variability made using the calendar for practical, seasonal predictions difficult. Correcting the calendar involved collecting better astronomical data and then using this data to make the necessary computations. This is what Omar did. It was an important contribution because his calendar was extremely accurate, and its accuracy made it extremely useful.

In the history of algebra, Omar Khayyám is best remembered for his work *Al-jabr w'al muqābala* (Demonstration concerning the completion and reduction of problems; this work is also known as Treatise on demonstration of problems of algebra). The *Al-jabr w'al muqābala* is heavily influenced by the ideas and works of Al-Khwārizmī, who had died two centuries before Omar wrote his algebra. As with al-Khwārizmī, Omar does not see all quadratic equations as instances of the single equation $ax^2 + bx + c = 0$. Instead, he, too, divides quadratic equations into distinct types, for example, "a number equals a square," which we would write as $x^2 = c$; "a square and roots equal a number," which we would write as $x^2 + bx = c$; and "a square and a number equal a root," which we would write $x^2 + c = x$. (He made a distinction, for example, between $x^2 + bx = c$ and $x^2 + c = bx$ because Omar, as do Diophantus and al-Khwārizmī, prefers to work with positive coefficients only.)

Omar even borrows al-Khwārizmī's examples. He uses the same equation, $x^2 = 5x$, that al-Khwārizmī used in his book, and there are the by-now standard geometric demonstrations involving the proofs of his algebraic results. All of this is familiar territory and would have seemed familiar even to al-Khwārizmī. But then Omar goes on to consider equations of the third degree—that is, equations of the form $ax^3 + bx^2 + cx + d = 0$.

Omar classifies third-degree equations by using the same general scheme that he used to classify equations of the second degree, and then he begins to try to solve them. He is unsuccessful in finding an algebraic method of obtaining a solution. He even states that one does not exist. (A method was discovered several centuries later in Europe.) Omar does, however, find a way to represent the solutions by using geometry, but his geometry is no longer the geometry of the Greeks. He has moved past traditional Euclidean geometry. Instead of using line segments as the Greeks had, Omar uses numbers to describe the properties of the curves in which he is interested. As he does so he broadens the subject of algebra and expands the collection of ideas and techniques that can be brought to bear on any problem.

Omar's synthesis of geometric and algebraic ideas is in some ways modern. When he discusses third-degree algebraic equations, equations that we would write as $ax^3 + bx^2 + cx + d = 0$, he represents his ideas geometrically. (Here a, b, c and d represent numbers and x is the unknown.) For example, the term x^3, "x cubed," is interpreted as a three-dimensional cube. This gives him a useful conceptual tool for understanding third-degree algebraic equations, but it also proves to be a barrier to further progress. The problem arises when he tries to extend his analysis to fourth-degree equations, equations that we would write as $ax^4 + bx^3 + cx^2 + dx + e = 0$. Because he cannot imagine a four-dimensional figure, his method fails him, and he questions the reality of equations of degree higher than 3.

To his credit Omar was aware of the close relationship between algebraic equations and the number system. However, his narrow concept of number prevented him from identifying many solutions that Hindu mathematicians accepted without question. This may seem to be a step backward, but his heightened sense of rigor was an important step forward. There are important relationships between the degree of an algebraic equation and the properties of the numbers that can appear as solutions. (The *degree* of an equation is the largest exponent that appears in it. Fourth-degree equations, for example, contain a variable raised to degree 4, and no higher power appears in the equation.) In fact, throughout much of the history of mathematics it was the study of algebraic equations that required mathematicians to consider more carefully their concept of what a number is and to search for ways in which the number system could be expanded to take into account the types of solutions that were eventually discovered. Omar's work in algebra would not be surpassed anywhere in the world for the next several centuries.

The work of al-Khwārizmī and Omar also exemplifies the best and most creative aspects of Islamic algebra. In particular, their synthesis of algebra and geometry allowed them to think about algebraic questions in a new way. Their worked yielded new insights into the relations that exist between algebra and geometry. They provided their successors with new tools to investigate algebra, and they attained a higher standard of rigor in the study of algebra. Although Indian mathematicians sometimes achieved more advanced results than their Islamic counterparts, Indian mathematicians tended to develop their mathematics via analogy or metaphor. These literary devices can be useful for discovering new aspects of mathematics, but they are of no use in separating the mathematically right from the mathematically wrong. Islamic mathematicians emphasized strong logical arguments—in fact, they seemed to enjoy them—and logically rigorous arguments are the only tools available for distinguishing the mathematically true from the mathematically false. It is in this sense that the algebra

LEONARDO OF PISA

There was one prominent European mathematician during the period in which Islamic mathematics flourished. He received his education in northern Africa from an Islamic teacher. As a consequence, he owed much of his insight to Islamic mathematics. He was the Italian mathematician Leonardo of Pisa, also known as Fibonacci (ca. 1170–after 1240). Leonardo's father, Guglielmo, was a government official in a Pisan community situated in what is now Algeria. During this time Leonardo studied mathematics with a Moor. (The Moors were an Islamic people who conquered Spain.) From his teacher he apparently learned both algebra and the Hindu base 10, place-value notation. He later wrote that he enjoyed the lessons. Those lessons also changed his life.

As a young man Leonardo traveled throughout North Africa and the Middle East. During his travels he learned about other systems of notation and other approaches to problem solving. He seems to have eventually settled down in Pisa, Italy, where he received a yearly income from the city.

Leonardo produced a number of works on mathematics. He described the place-value notation and advocated for its adoption. His efforts helped to spread news of the system throughout Europe. (Leonardo only used place-value notation to express whole numbers. He did not use the decimal notation to write fractions.) His description of the Indian system of notation is his most long-lasting contribution, but he also discovered what is now known as the Fibonacci series, and he was renowned for his skill in algebra as well. He studied, for example, the equation that we would write as $x^3 + 2x^2 + 10x = 20$. This equation was taken from the work of Omar Khayyám. In his analysis Leonardo apparently recognizes that the solution he sought was not a simple whole number or fraction. He responds by working out an approximation—and he recognizes that his answer *is* an approximation—that is accurate to the ninth decimal place. Leonardo, however, expressed his answer as a base 60 fraction. Unfortunately Leonardo does not explain how he found his answer, an approximation that would set the European standard for accuracy for the next several centuries.

developed by the Islamic mathematicians is—especially during the period bracketed by the lives of al-Khwārizmī and Omar—much closer to a modern conception of algebra than is that of the Indians.

4

ALGEBRA AS A THEORY
OF EQUATIONS

As art, music, literature, and science did, mathematics flourished in Europe during the Renaissance, which had its origins in 14th-century Italy and spread throughout Europe over the succeeding three centuries. Just as art, music, and science changed radically during the Renaissance, all pre-Renaissance mathematics is profoundly different from the post-Renaissance mathematics of Europe. The new mathematics began with discoveries in algebra.

Many of the best European mathematicians of this period were still strongly influenced by the algebra of al-Khwārizmī, but in the space of a few years Italian mathematicians went far beyond all of the algorithms for solving equations that had been discovered anywhere since the days of the Mesopotamians. Mathematicians found solutions to whole classes of algebraic equations that had never been solved before. Their methods of solution were, by our standards, excessively complicated. The algorithms developed by Renaissance era mathematicians were also difficult and sometimes even counterintuitive. A lack of insight into effective notation, poor mathematical technique, and an inadequate understanding of what a number is sometimes made recognizing that they had found a solution difficult for them. Nevertheless, many problems were solved for the first time, and this was important, because these problems had resisted solution for thousands of years.

The new algorithms also exposed large gaps in the understanding of these mathematicians. To close those gaps they would have to expand their concept of number, their collection of problem solving techniques, and their algebraic notation. The algebraic solution of these new classes of problems was a major event in the history of mathematics. In fact, many historians believe that the modern era in mathematics begins with publication of the Renaissance era algebra book *Ars Magna*, about which we will have much more to say later.

To appreciate what these Renaissance era mathematicians accomplished, we begin by examining a simple example. The example is a quadratic equation, an algebraic equation of second degree. The remarks we make about quadratic equations guide our discussion of the more complicated equations and formulas used by the mathematicians of the Renaissance. Our example is taken from the work of al-Khwārizmī. He was an expert at this type of problem, but because his description is a little old-fashioned, and because we also want to discuss his problem in modern notation, we introduce a little terminology first. A quadratic, or second-degree, equation is any equation that we can write in the form $ax^2 + bx + c = 0$. In this equation, the letter x is the variable. The number or numbers that, when substituted for x, make the equation a true statement are called the *roots* of the equation, and the equation is solved when we find the root or roots. The letters a, b, and c are the *coefficients*. They represent numbers that we assume are known. In the following excerpt, al-Khwārizmī is describing his method of solving the equation $x^2 + 21 = 10x$. In this example the coefficient a equals 1. The coefficient b is -10. (Al-Khwārizmī prefers to transpose the term $-10x$ to the right side of the equation because he does not work with negative coefficients.) Finally, the c coefficient equals 21. Here is al-Khwārizmī's method for solving the equation $x^2 + 21 = 10x$:

> A square and 21 units equal 10 roots. . . . The solution of this type of problem is obtained in the following manner. You take first one-half of the roots, giving in this instance 5, which multiplied by itself gives 25. From 25 subtract the 21 units to which we have just referred in connection with the squares. This gives 4, of which you extract the square root, which is 2. From the half of

the roots, or 5, you take 2 away, and 3 remains, constituting one root of this square which itself is, of course, 9.

(Al-Khwārizmī, Mohammed ibn-Mūsā. Robert of Chester's Latin Translation of the Algebra of al-Khwārizmī. *Translated by Karpinski, Louis C. New York: The Macmillan Company, 1915)*

Al-Khwārizmī has given a rhetorical description of an application of the algorithm called the quadratic formula. Notice that what al-Khwārizmī is doing is "constructing" the root, or solution of the equation, from a formula that uses the coefficients of the equation as input. Once he has identified the coefficients he can, with the help of his formula, compute the root. We do the same thing when we use the quadratic formula, although both our formula and our concept of solution are more general than those of al-Khwārizmī. In fact, we learn two formulas when we learn to solve equations of the form $ax^2 + bx + c = 0$. The first is

$$x = \frac{-b}{2a} + \frac{\sqrt{b^2-4ac}}{2a},$$ and the second is $x = \frac{-b}{2a} - \frac{\sqrt{b^2-4ac}}{2a}$. These are

the formulas that allow us to identify the roots of a quadratic equation provided we know the coefficients.

Various rhetorical forms of these formulas were known to al-Khwārizmī and even to Mesopotamian mathematicians. They are useful for finding roots of second-degree equations, but they are useless for computing the roots of an equation whose degree is not 2. Until the Renaissance, *no one in the history of humankind* had found corresponding formulas for equations of degree higher than 2. No one had found a formula comparable to the quadratic formula for a third-degree equation, that is, an equation of the form $ax^3 + bx^2 + cx + d = 0$, where a, b, c, and d are the coefficients. This was one of the great achievements of the Renaissance.

There is one more point to notice about the preceding formulas for determining the solutions to the second-degree equations: They are exact. These formulas leave no uncertainty at all about the true value for x. We can compare these formulas with the solution that Leonardo of Pisa obtained for the third-degree equation given in the preceding chapter. His approximation was accurate to the billionth place. This is far more accurate than he (or we) would need for any practical application, but there is still some uncertainty about the true value for *x*.

From a practical point of view, Leonardo completely solved the problem, but from a theoretical point of view, there is an important distinction between his answer and the exact answer. His approximation is a rational number. It can be expressed as a quotient of two whole numbers. The exact answer, the number that he was searching for, is an irrational number. It *cannot* be expressed as a quotient of two whole numbers. Leonardo's solution was, for the time, a prodigious feat of calculation, but it fails to communicate some of the mathematically interesting features of the exact solution. Leonardo's work shows us that even during the Middle Ages there were algorithms that enabled one to compute highly accurate *approximations* to at least some equations of the third degree, but there was no general algorithm for obtaining exact solutions to equations of the third degree.

The New Algorithms

The breakthrough that occurred in Renaissance Italy was unrelated to finding useful approximations to algebraic equations. It involved the discovery of an algorithm for obtaining exact solutions of algebraic equations.

The discovery of exact algorithms for equations of degree higher than 2 begins with an obscure Italian academic named Scipione del Ferro (1465–1526). Little is known of del Ferro, nor are scholars sure about precisely what he discovered. Some historians believe that he was educated at the University of Bologna, but there are no records that indicate that he was. What is certain is that in 1496 he joined the faculty at the University of Bologna as a lecturer in arithmetic and geometry and that he remained at the university for the rest of his life.

Uncertainty about del Ferro's precise contribution to the history of algebra arises from the fact that he did not publish his ideas and discoveries about mathematics. He was not secretive. He apparently shared his discoveries with friends. Evidently he learned how to solve certain types of cubic equations. These equations had resisted exact solution for thousands of years, so del Ferro's discovery was a momentous one. Del Ferro did not learn how to solve every cubic equation, however.

As their Islamic predecessors had not, the European mathematicians of del Ferro's time did not use negative coefficients, so they did not perceive a cubic equation as a single case as we do today. Today we say that a cubic equation is *any* equation that can be written in the form $ax^3 + bx^2 + cx + d = 0$. But where we see unity, they saw a diversity of types of cubic equations. They classified equations by the side of the equals sign where each coefficient was written. Where we would write a negative coefficient they carefully transposed the term containing the negative coefficient to the other side of the equation so that the only coefficients they considered were positive. For example, they looked at the equations $x^3 + 2x = 1$ and $x^3 = 2x + 1$ as separate cases. Furthermore, they would also consider any cubic equation with an x^2 term, such as $x^3 + 3x^2 = 1$, as a case separate from, say, $x^3 + 2x = 1$, because the former has an x^2 term and no x term, whereas the latter equation has an x term but no x^2 term. The number of such separate cases for a third-degree equation is quite large.

Although we cannot be sure exactly what types of cubic equations del Ferro solved, many scholars believe that he learned to solve one or both of the following types of third-degree algebraic equations: (1) $x^3 + cx = d$ and/or (2) $x^3 = cx + d$, where in each equation the letters c and d represent positive numbers. Whatever del Ferro learned, he passed it on to one of his students, Antonio Maria Fior.

News of del Ferro's discovery eventually reached the ears of a young, creative, and ambitious mathematician and scientist named Niccolò Fontana (1499–1557), better known as Tartaglia. Tartaglia was born in the city of Brescia, which is located in what is now northern Italy. It was a place of great wealth when Tartaglia was a boy, but Tartaglia did not share in that wealth. His father, a postal courier, died when Tartaglia was young, and the family was left in poverty. It is often said that Tartaglia was self-taught. In one story the 14-year-old Tartaglia hires a tutor to help him learn to read but has only enough money to reach the letter k. In 1512, when Tartaglia was barely a teenager, the city was sacked by the French. There were widespread looting and violence. Tartaglia suffered severe saber wounds to his face, wounds that left him with a permanent speech impediment. (Tartaglia, a name which he took as his own, began as a nickname. It means "stammerer.")

When Tartaglia heard the news that del Ferro had discovered a method of solving certain third-degree equations, he began the search for

Niccolò Fontana, also known as Tartaglia. His discovery of a method to solve arbitrary third-degree equations had a profound effect on the history of mathematics. (Library of Congress, Prints and Photographs Division)

his own method of solving those equations. What he discovered was a method for solving equations of the form $x^3 + px^2 = q$. Notice that this is a different type of equation from those that had been solved by using del Ferro's method, but both algorithms have something important in common: They enable the user to construct solution(s) using only the coefficients that appear in the equation itself. Tartaglia and del Ferro had found formulas for third-degree equations that were similar in concept to the quadratic formula.

When Tartaglia announced his discovery, a contest was arranged between him and del Ferro's student, Antonio Maria Fior. Each mathematician provided the other with a list of problems, and each was required to solve the other's equations within a specified time. Although he initially encountered some difficulty, Tartaglia soon discovered how to extend his algorithm to solve those types of problems proposed by Fior, but Fior did not discover how to solve the types of problems proposed by Tartaglia. It was a great triumph for Tartaglia.

Tartaglia did not stop with his discoveries in algebra. He also wrote a physics book, *Nova Scientia* (A new science), in which he tried to establish the physical laws governing bodies in free fall, a subject that would soon play an important role in the history of science and mathematics. Tartaglia had established himself as an important mathematician and scientist. He was on his way up.

It is at this point that the exploits of the Italian gambler, physician, mathematician, philosopher, and astrologer Girolamo Cardano (1501–76) become important to Tartaglia and the history of science. Unlike del Ferro, who published nothing, Cardano published numerous books describing his ideas, his philosophies, and his insights on every subject that aroused his curiosity, and he was a very curious man. He published the first book on probability. As a physician he published the first clinical description of typhus, a serious disease that is transmitted through the bite of certain insects. He also wrote about philosophy, and he seemed to enjoy writing about himself as well. His autobiography is entitled *De Propria Vita* (Book of my life). In the field of algebra, Cardano did two things of great importance: He wrote the book *Ars Magna* (Great art), the book that many historians believe marks the start of the modern era in mathematics, and he helped an impoverished boy named Lodovico Ferrari (1522–65).

Tartaglia also helped to invent the science of ballistics. Extending from the cannon is his invention, the gun quadrant. (Library of Congress, Prints and Photographs Division)

At the age of 14 Ferrari applied to work for Cardano as a servant, but unlike most servants of the time, Ferrari could read and write.

Impressed, Cardano hired him as his personal secretary instead. It soon became apparent to Cardano that his young secretary had great potential, so Cardano made sure that Ferrari received an excellent university education. Ferrari learned Greek, Latin, and mathematics at the university where Cardano lectured, and when Ferrari was 18, Cardano resigned his post at the university in favor of his former secretary. At the age of 18 Ferrari was lecturing in mathematics at the University of Milan. Together Cardano and Ferrari would soon make an important contribution to mathematics.

Meanwhile Tartaglia's success had attracted Cardano's attention. Although Tartaglia had discovered how to solve cubic equations, he had not made his algorithm public. He preferred to keep it secret. Cardano wanted to know the secret. Initially he sent a letter requesting information about the algorithm, but Tartaglia refused the request. Cardano, a capable mathematician in his own right and a very persistent person, did not give up. He continued to write to Tartaglia. They argued. Still Tartaglia would not tell, and still Cardano persisted. Their positions, however, were not equal. Tartaglia, though well known, was not well off. By contrast, Cardano was wealthy and well connected. He indicated that he could help Tartaglia find a prestigious position, which Tartaglia very much wanted. Cardano invited Tartaglia to his home, and, in exchange for a promise that Cardano would tell no one, Tartaglia shared his famous algorithm with his host.

It was a mistake, of course. Tartaglia is said to have recognized his error almost as soon as he made it. Cardano was of no help in finding Tartaglia a position, but with the solution to the third-degree equation firmly in hand, Cardano asked his former servant, secretary, and pupil, Ferrari, to solve the general fourth-degree equation, and Ferrari, full of energy and insight, did as he was asked. He discovered a formula that enabled the user to construct the root(s) to a fourth-degree equation by using only the coefficients that appeared in the equation itself. Now Cardano knew how to solve both third- and fourth-degree equations, and that is the information Cardano published in *Ars Magna*.

Tartaglia was furious. He and Cardano exchanged accusations and insults. The whole fight was very public, and much of the public was fascinated. Eventually a debate was arranged between Tartaglia and Ferrari, who was an intensely loyal man who never forgot who gave him help when he needed it. It was a long debate, and it did not go well for Tartaglia. The debate was not finished when Tartaglia left. He did not return. Tartaglia felt betrayed and remained angry about the affair for the rest of his life.

Girolamo Cardano, author of Ars Magna, *one of the great mathematical works of his era.* (Library of Congress, Prints and Photographs Division)

In some ways Cardano's *Ars Magna* is an old-fashioned book. It is written very much in the style of al-Khwārizmī: It is a purely rhetorical work, long on prose and bereft of algebraic notation. That is one reason that it is both tedious and difficult for a modern reader to follow. In the manner of al-Khwārizmī, Cardano avoids negative coefficients by transposing terms to one side of the equation or another until all the numbers appearing in the equation are nonnegative. In this sense, *Ars Magna* belongs to an earlier age.

The significance of *Ars Magna* lies in three areas. First, the solutions that arose in the course of applying the new algorithms were often of a very complicated nature. For example, numbers such as

$$\sqrt[3]{287\frac{1}{2}+\sqrt{80449\frac{1}{4}}} + \sqrt[3]{287\frac{1}{2}-\sqrt{80449\frac{1}{4}}} - 5,$$ a solution that Cardano

derives in his book for a fourth-degree equation, inspired many mathematicians to reconsider their ideas of what a number is. This turned out to be a very difficult problem to resolve, but with the new algorithms, it was no longer possible to avoid asking the question.

ALGEBRA AS A TOOL IN SCIENCE

During the Renaissance great progress was made in obtaining exact solutions to algebraic equations. There was a certain excitement associated with the work of Tartaglia, Ferrari, and others because these mathematicians were solving problems that had resisted solution for millennia. There was also a highly abstract quality to their work: It was now possible to solve fourth-degree equations, for example, but opportunities to use fourth-degree equations to solve practical problems were not especially numerous.

Galileo Galilei. Algebraic ideas are present in some of Galileo's mathematical descriptions of his work, but he expresses himself rhetorically—without any specialized algebraic notation. This makes his ideas somewhat difficult to read. (Library of Congress, Prints and Photographs Division)

There was, however, another trend that was occurring during the Renaissance, the application of algebra to the solution of problems in science. There is no better example of a scientist's reliance on algebra as a language in which to express ideas than in the work of the Italian scientist, mathematician, and inventor Galileo Galilei (1564–1642). Galileo's algebraic approach broke with the past. Archimedes, Aristarchus of Samos, and other Greek scientists and mathematicians often used straightedge and compass geometry to express many of their ideas. For well over 1,000 years geometry had been the language of scientific inquiry. This began to change during the Renaissance.

One of Galileo's best-known books, *Dialogues Concerning Two New Sciences,* is filled with algebra. It is not a book about algebra. It is a book about science, in which Galileo discusses the great scientific topics of his time: motion, strength of materials, levers, and other topics that lie at the heart of classical mechanics. To express his scientific ideas he uses a rhetorical version of an algebraic function.

In the following quotation, taken from *Dialogues,* Galileo is describing discoveries he had made about the ability of objects to resist fracture:

(continues)

ALGEBRA AS A TOOL IN SCIENCE
(continued)

Prisms and cylinders which differ in both length and thickness offer resistances to fracture . . . which are directly proportional to the cubes of the diameters of their bases and inversely proportional to their lengths.

(Galileo Galilei. Dialogues Concerning Two New Sciences. *Translated by Henry Crew and Alfonso de Salvio. New York: Dover Publications, 1954)*

Galileo is describing the physical characteristics of real objects with algebraic functions. Unfortunately he lacks a convenient algebraic notation to express these ideas.

In his use of algebra, Galileo was not alone. During the Renaissance scientists discovered that algebra was often the most convenient way that they had to express their ideas. The synthesis that occurred between algebra and science during the Renaissance accelerated interest in algebra. It probably also accelerated progress in science because it made new abstract relations between different properties more transparent and easier to manipulate. Algebra *as a symbolic language* was gaining prominence in mathematics. As notation improved and insight deepened into how algebra could be used, algebraic notation became the standard way that mathematicians expressed their ideas in many branches of mathematics. Today algebra has so thoroughly permeated the language of mathematics and the physical sciences that it is doubtful that the subject matter of these important disciplines could be expressed independently of the algebraic notation in which they are written.

Second, Cardano's book marks the first time since the Mesopotamians began pressing their ideas about quadratic equations into clay slabs that anyone had published general methods for obtaining exact solutions to equations higher than second degree. Algebra had always seemed to hold a lot of promise, but its actual utility had been limited because mathematicians knew only enough algebra to solve relatively simple problems. The problems that were solved by the Mesopotamian, Chinese, Indian, and Islamic mathematicians were by and large simple variations on a very small group of very similar problems. This changed with the publication of *Ars Magna*.

Finally, Cardano's book made it seem at least possible that similar formulas might exist for algebraic equations of fifth degree and higher. This possibility inspired many mathematicians to begin searching for algorithms that would enable them to find exact solutions for equations of degree higher than 4.

François Viète, Algebra as a Symbolic Language

Inspired by the very public success of Tartaglia and Ferrari and the book of Cardano, the study of algebra spread throughout much of Europe. One of the first and most obvious barriers to further progress was the lack of a convenient symbolism for expressing the new ideas, but this condition was changing, albeit in a haphazard way. Throughout Europe various algebraic symbols were introduced. Mathematicians in different geographical or linguistic regions employed different notation. There were several symbols proposed for what we now know as an equals sign (=). There were also alternatives for +, −, ×, and so on. It took time for the notation to become standardized, but all of these notational innovations were important in the sense that they made algebra easier. Rhetorical algebra can be slow to read and unnecessarily difficult to follow. Ordinary everyday language, the kind of language that we use in conversation, is just not the right language in which to express algebra, and the higher the level of abstraction becomes, the more difficult the rhetorical expression of algebra is to read. Nor was the lack of a suitable notation the only barrier to progress.

Algebra is about more than symbols. Algebra is about ideas, and despite the creativity of del Ferro, Tartaglia, Ferrari, and others, the algebra of much of the 16th century was similar in concept to what Islamic mathematicians had developed centuries earlier. For most mathematicians of the time, algebra was still about finding roots of equations. It was a very concrete subject. The equation was like a question; the numbers that satisfied the equation were the answers. A successful mathematician could solve several different types of equations; an unsuccessful mathematician could not. At the time algebra was a collection of problem-solving techniques. It was the search for formulas. The formulas might well be complicated, of course, but the goal was not. This view of algebra is a very narrow one. In the end it is a view of algebra that is not even very productive. One of the first mathematicians to understand that algebra is about more than developing techniques to solve equations was the French mathematician François Viète (1540–1603).

Viète was born into a comfortable family in Fontenay-le-Comte, a small town located in the west of France not far from the Bay of Biscay. He studied law at the University of Poitiers. Perhaps his initial interest in law was due to his father, who was also a lawyer, but the legal profession was not for Viète. Within a few years of graduation he had given up on law and was working as a tutor for a wealthy family. His work as a tutor was a quiet beginning to an eventful life. As that of many French citizens was, Viète's life was profoundly influenced by the political instability that long plagued France. During Viète's life the cause of the turmoil was religious tension between the Roman Catholic majority and the Protestant minority, called Huguenots. Viète's sympathies lay with the Huguenots.

While he was working as a tutor, Viète began his research into mathematics. He left his job as a tutor in 1573, when he was appointed to a government position. Fortunately for mathematics, in 1584 he was banished from government for his Huguenot sympathies. Viète moved to a small town and for five years devoted himself to the study of mathematics. It was, mathematically speaking, the most productive time of his life.

Viète understood that the unknowns in an algebraic equation could represent *types* of objects. His was a much broader view of an equation than simply as an opportunity to find "the answer." If the unknown could represent a type or "species" of object, then algebra was about the relationships between types. Viète's higher level of abstract thought led to an important notational breakthrough. It is to Viète that we owe the idea of representing the unknown in an equation with a letter. In fact, in his search for more general patterns Viète also used letters to represent known quantities as well. (The "known quantities" are what we have been calling coefficients.) Although we have been using this notation since the beginning of this volume—it is hard to talk about algebra without it—historically speaking, this method of notation did not begin until Viète invented it.

Viète's method was to use vowels to represent unknown quantities and consonants to represent known quantities. This is not quite what we use today; today we let letters toward the end of the alphabet represent unknowns and letters toward the beginning of the alphabet represent known quantities, but it is the first instance of the concept. Notice that by employing letters for the coefficients Viète deprives himself of any hope of finding numerical solutions. The compensation for this loss of specificity is that the letters made it easier for Viète to see broader patterns. The letters helped him identify relationships between the various symbols and the classes of objects that they represented.

Though some of Viète's ideas were important and innovative, others were old-fashioned or just plain awkward. Viète was old-fashioned in that he still had a fairly restricted idea of what constituted an acceptable solution. As had his predecessors, Viète accepted only positive numbers as legitimate solutions.

Viète had an unusual and, in retrospect, awkward idea for how unknowns and coefficients should be combined. He interpreted his unknowns as if there were units attached to them. We have already encountered a similar sort of interpretation. Recall that Omar Khayyám had conceptual difficulties in dealing with fourth-degree equations *because* he interpreted an unknown as a length. For Omar an unknown length squared represented a (geometric) square, an unknown length cubed was a (three-dimensional) cube, and as a consequence there was no immediate way of interpreting an unknown raised to the fourth power. In a similar vein, Viète required all terms in an equation to be "homogeneous" in the sense that they all had to have the same units. The equation that we would write as $x^2 + x = 1$, an equation without dimensions, would have made little sense to Viète since it involved adding, for example, a line segment, x, to a square, x^2. Instead Viète insisted on assigning dimensions to his coefficients so that all terms had the same dimensions. For example, he preferred to work with equations like $A^3 - 3B^2A = B^2D$. This was very important to him, although in retrospect it is hard to see why. Succeeding generations of mathematicians perceived his requirement of homogeneity as a hindrance and abandoned it.

Viète's work was a remarkable mixture of the old and the new, and with these conceptual tools he began to develop a theory of equations. Although he knew how to solve all algebraic equations up to and including those of the fourth degree, he went further than simply identifying the roots. He was, for example, able to identify certain cases in which the coefficients that appeared in the equations were functions of the equation's solutions. This is, in a sense, the reverse of the problem considered by Tartaglia and Ferrari, who found formulas that gave the solutions as functions of the coefficients. This observation allowed Viète to begin making new connections between the coefficients that appeared in the equation and the roots of the equation.

Viète also began to notice relationships between the degree of the equation and the number of roots of the equation. He demonstrated that at least in certain cases, the number of roots was the same as the degree of the equation. (He was prevented from drawing more general conclusions by his narrow conception of what a number, and hence a solution, is.)

All of these observations are important because there are many connections between the solutions of an algebraic equation and the form of the equation. It turns out that if one knows the coefficients and the degree of the equation then one also knows a great deal about the roots, and vice versa. Then as now the exact solutions (roots) of an equation were sometimes less important to mathematicians than other, more abstract properties of the equation itself. Viète may well have been the first mathematician to think along these lines.

Viète eventually had the opportunity to return to government, but he did not abandon his mathematical studies. His mathematical skill proved useful in his service to King Henry IV, when he decrypted a number of secret messages sent by the king of Spain during a religious war. The code was, for the time, state of the art, and the Spanish believed it to be unbreakable. Viète's success caused the Spanish king to complain to the pope that the French had used sorcery to decrypt the messages. Viète was also interested in astronomy, and he wrote a long and unpublished work comparing the geometries of the Ptolemaic and Copernican systems. As did any good astronomer of the time he also needed to know trigonometry, and in his book *Canon Mathematicus Seu ad Triangula* (Mathematical laws applied to triangles), he helped to develop that field as well.

More importantly for the history of algebra, Viète also wrote about the three classical, unsolved problems of ancient Greece: trisection of an angle, squaring of a circle, and doubling of a cube. During Viète's life, interest in the problems again became fashionable, and claims were made that all three problems had finally been solved via straightedge and compass. Viète rightly showed that all the new proofs were faulty and that the problems remained unsolved. Finally a Belgian mathematician had found a way to solve one particular algebraic equation of degree 45. An ambassador from that region to the court of Henry IV boasted of the skill of the mathematicians of his homeland. He said that there were no mathematicians in France capable of solving such a difficult problem. The job of defending the French national honor fell to Viète. Using trigonometric methods, Viète, too, found a way to solve the problem.

Viète, a lawyer by training, was perhaps the most forward-thinking and capable mathematician of his time. If he had one rival anywhere in Europe, it was the British mathematician and astronomer Thomas Harriot.

Thomas Harriot

Very little is known of Thomas Harriot (1560–1621) before he enrolled in Oxford University. After he graduated from Oxford, his life becomes much easier to trace because his fortunes became intertwined with those of Sir Walter Raleigh (ca. 1554–1618). Today Sir Walter Raleigh is best remembered as a swashbuckling adventurer and a writer. He sailed the Atlantic Ocean, freely confusing the national good with his own personal profit. He attempted to establish a colony on Roanoke Island in present-day North Carolina, and he sailed to present-day Guyana in search of gold to loot. He wrote about his adventures, and his exploits made him a popular figure with the general public and with Queen Elizabeth I.

As a favorite of the queen, Raleigh was granted a number of opportunities to amass great wealth, and he seems to have taken advantage of all of them. Less well known is that Sir Walter Raleigh was also a serious student of mathematics. He was not an especially insightful mathematician himself, but he hired Thomas Harriot, who was probably the best mathematician in England at the time, a decision that displayed sound mathematical judgment.

Raleigh's interest in mathematics was not purely scholarly. He was hoping that the application of mathematics to problems in navigation would enable mariners to determine their position on the sea more accurately. This interest in better navigational techniques and tools also accounted for much of his interest in Harriot.

Thomas Harriot spent much of his time working on mathematical problems that were of interest to Raleigh. He researched the question of how best to use observations of the Sun and stars to determine one's latitude accurately. He worked as a naval architect and an accountant for Raleigh, and he was busy with other nonmathematical

An imprisoned Sir Walter Raleigh says good-bye to his wife. Harriot's fortunes were closely tied to those of Raleigh, his patron. Harriot prospered when Raleigh did, but when Raleigh was imprisoned and later executed, Harriot lost support and was briefly imprisoned himself. (Library of Congress, Prints and Photographs Division)

pursuits that also arose out of his association with Raleigh. He sailed to Virginia, for example, on a trip arranged by Raleigh. While there he learned the Algonquian language and served as interpreter and spokesman for his group.

As a scientist Harriot had interests that were very broad. He was an avid astronomer and built several telescopes of his own. He studied optics and chemistry in addition to algebra. He even had personal and professional knowledge of Viète through his good friend Nathaniel Torporley, who was for a time secretary to Viète. Mathematically Harriot was more modern in outlook than Viète. In contrast to that of Viète, who, as we have already mentioned, used a complicated mix of symbols and words, Harriot's algebraic notation was simpler and, consequently, more modern. He also had a much broader concept of what a number is than Viète. Harriot accepted positive, negative, and imaginary roots as solutions, although as all mathematicians for the next few hundred years had, Harriot had only a fuzzy idea of what an imaginary number, in fact, was.

In the field of algebra Harriot made an important observation about the relationship between the solutions to an equation and the equation itself. To understand the idea, recall that Mesopotamian, Greek, Chinese, Indian, and Islamic mathematicians had always been concerned with the problem of finding solutions to a given equation. This was also the goal of the Italian mathematicians of the Renaissance. We can call this the forward problem; Harriot gave some thought to what we might call the inverse problem: Suppose we are given three solutions to a single algebraic equation, can we find an algebraic equation of degree 3 with these numbers as solutions? Harriot discovered that the answer is yes, and that the solution is simple. Suppose that a, b, and c are the three given roots. The equation, expressed in modern notation, is $(x - a)(x - b)(x - c) = 0$. The terms in parentheses are *linear factors*. To see this third-degree polynomial—which has a, b, and c as roots—in the form to which we have become accustomed, we simply multiply the three linear factors together.

To appreciate Harriot's insight, recall that the product of a set of numbers can only be 0 if at least one of the numbers is 0.

Therefore Harriot's equation is only satisfied if x is equal to a, or b, or c. This guarantees that the expression on the left, which is written as a product of linear factors, has *only* a, b, and c as roots. Furthermore if the three terms on the left side of the equation are multiplied together, the coefficients of the third-degree equation are expressed as functions of a, b, and c. When we multiply the terms out we get $x^3 - (a + b + c)x^2 + (ab + bc + ac)x - abc = 0$. This shows, for example, that the coefficient of the x^2 term is the sum of the roots of the equation and that the last term on the left is the product of the roots. By considering the inverse problem, Harriot was able to discover a number of facts about algebraic equations that could have proved helpful to other mathematicians interested in these problems.

Unfortunately Harriot had little influence on his contemporaries. Initially he did not seem to have much interest in communicating his ideas to a wider audience. Later political problems took up much of his time. Politically he ran into problems that resulted from his association with Sir Walter Raleigh. When Queen Elizabeth I died, the throne was assumed by King James I. The new king did not approve of Raleigh's adventurism. Later Raleigh and others were accused of trying to overthrow James. Raleigh was imprisoned. Meanwhile Harriot had found a new patron and continued his scientific research. Raleigh was eventually freed from prison, but later he was rearrested and eventually executed. The decisions that had ruled against Raleigh had tarnished Harriot as well. Eventually Harriot's new patron was imprisoned. Even Harriot spent a little time in prison. In addition to his essentially political problems, Harriot's health began to fail him. A cancer slowly robbed him of his energy, and still his mathematical ideas lay in drawers and on tables in his study. These papers represented 40 years of work in science and mathematics, and nothing had been published. It was only when Harriot was on his deathbed, dying of cancer, that he finally addressed the question of the publication of his mathematical works. He requested that his lifelong friend Nathaniel Torporley sort through his papers and assemble his work so that it might finally be published. It was one of the last requests he made, but Torporley never did apply himself to the task. Another longtime friend of Harriot eventually assembled a single slim book for publication. It was entitled *Artis Analyticae Praxis*, now called the *Praxis*, and it is through this single effort that we now know of Harriot's accomplishments in algebra.

Albert Girard and the Fundamental Theorem of Algebra

It was near the end of Harriot's life that the Flemish mathematician Albert Girard (1590–1633) was most active in mathematics. Today he is remembered for an interesting observation—but not a proof—about the nature of algebraic equations. His observation was only speculation, and, as we will soon see, there were many difficulties to be resolved before a proof would become possible, but Girard's musings demonstrated considerable insight into the nature of algebraic equations.

Not much is written about Girard today. Even in his own time he was generally referred to as an engineer rather than a mathematician because of his accomplishments as a military architect, designing fortifications and the like. We do know that he attended the University of Leiden, in Holland, and that he worked for a time with the Flemish scientist, mathematician, and engineer Simon Stevin. Girard's best-known book is *Invention nouvelle en l'algèbre*, and much of the work is of an evolutionary rather than revolutionary character. He extends the work of Viète on several fronts. He applies trigonometric methods to the solution of algebraic equations, in itself an extension of some work done by Viète, and he also extends Viète's ideas on the relationship between roots and coefficients in an algebraic equation.

Girard's most interesting contribution was his speculation that every polynomial of degree n has n roots. Neither al-Khwārizmī nor Viète could have made this assertion because they accepted only positive roots as valid roots. For them, it was false that every polynomial of degree n had n roots. In order for the statement to be true one must have a much broader idea of what constitutes a number. Even Girard had only a hazy idea of what a complex number was; that is one reason why his assertion is little more than guesswork. It is, nevertheless, an insightful guess, which, together with the corresponding proof, is called the fundamental theorem of algebra.

To understand the meaning of Girard's guess, consider the following analogy with the set of natural numbers. The set of natural numbers, which is just another name for the set of positive whole numbers, can be divided into three groups: prime numbers, composite numbers, and the number 1. (The number 1 constitutes its own class. It is neither prime nor composite.) The prime numbers are divisible only by themselves and 1. For example, the first four prime numbers are 2, 3, 5, and 7. Any natural number other than 1 that is not prime is called a composite number. Composite numbers are always divisible by at least one prime number. For example, the composite number 462 can be written as the product of four primes: $462 = 2 \times 3 \times 7 \times 11$. One consequence of this observation about divisibility is that it is always possible to write any natural number greater than 1 as a product of prime numbers. It is in this sense that the prime numbers are like building blocks. Any natural number greater than 1 can be "constructed" by multiplying the right primes together.

Essentially Girard speculated that linear factors, expressions of the form $(x - a)$ act as prime numbers. As noted previously, we call these simple, first-degree polynomials linear factors. Girard thought that it was possible to represent *every* polynomial as a product of linear factors. To be specific, suppose we are given a polynomial of the form $x^n + a_{n-1}x^{n-1} + \ldots + a_1x + a_0$. (Recall that x^j is the variable x raised to the jth power, and a_j is the rational number by which we multiply x^j.) Girard's assertion is equivalent to saying that it is possible to find n linear factors $(x - r_1)$, $(x - r_2)$, $(x - r_3)$, $\ldots$, $(x - r_n)$ such that when we multiply them together we get $x^n + a_{n-1}x^{n-1} + \ldots + a_1x + a_0$, and where the r_js are the roots of the polynomial. In this sense, every polynomial of degree greater than 1 plays the role of a composite number in the set of all polynomials, and every linear factor—that is, the set of polynomials of degree 1—functions as the set of prime numbers does. Essentially Girard speculated that it should, in theory, be possible to factor

$$x^n + a_{n-1}x^n + a_{n-2}x^{n-2} + \ldots + a_1x + a_0 = (x-r_1)(x-r_2)(x-r_3)\ldots(x-r_n)$$

Girard hypothesized that every polynomial of degree n has n roots. This is equivalent to the hypothesis that every polynomial of degree n can be written as a product of n linear factors.

every polynomial into a product of linear factors in the same way that we can factor every composite number into a product of primes.

Girard was not the only mathematician of the time to think along these lines. Harriot discovered a simple case of this idea when he investigated cubic equations, and even Viète seems to have had some hazy ideas about the matter, but Girard was the first to see the big picture. These were new and fundamental ideas about the nature of algebraic equations, and they would occupy the imagination of many mathematicians for the next two centuries.

With the work of del Ferro, Tartaglia, and Ferrari, on the one hand, and that of Viète, Harriot, and Girard, on the other, mathematicians interested in algebra were faced with two different avenues for further research. One avenue was to look for exact solutions to algebraic equations of the fifth degree and higher. The second avenue of research was to examine Girard's more fundamental assertion about the structure of the equations themselves.

At the outset both roads must have looked equally promising, but time would prove otherwise. Although the existence of general formulas for the roots of equations of the second, third, and fourth degree pointed to the possibility of similar formulas for equations of even higher degree, it was eventually discovered that no other general formulas exist. This is not the same as saying that the formulas have not yet been found. The algorithms were not found because they *cannot* be found. They do not exist. The nonexistence of general formulas, written in terms of the coefficients, for equations of degree higher than 4 was something of a surprise. The proof would depend on deep, new concepts, and developing them would take work and time. Proving that the sought-after formulas do not exist would have to wait a few centuries. The other possibility for research, that of a deeper look at the structure of algebraic equations, would prove very fruitful and would occupy some of the best minds in mathematics.

To go beyond Girard's speculations and probe more deeply into the nature of algebraic equations, mathematicians had to consider two fundamental questions. The first difficulty to overcome was to determine whether it is even possible to represent every polynomial as a product of linear factors, that is, factors of the form $x - a$, where a represents a root of the equation. The second, related problem that had to be confronted involved the number system to which the a's belonged: *If* it was possible to write any polynomial as a product of linear factors, what type(s) of numbers would appear in place of the a's in the linear factors? Mathematicians had already established that even in the case of second-degree equations, the real numbers were not sufficient. For example, there is no real number that satisfies the equation $x^2 + 1 = 0$. The only solutions to this equation are $+i$ and $-i$, where i represents a complex number with the property that i^2 equals -1.

Many early attempts to establish the nature of the roots of an algebraic equation failed because mathematicians simply assumed that Girard was correct when he speculated that the polynomial could be factored. But any "proof" that *assumes* that a polynomial can be written as a product of linear factors and then goes on to *prove* that the roots must be complex numbers cannot be accepted as a valid proof. If it has not been established that the polynomial can be written as a product of linear factors, then we cannot accept any conclusions regarding the nature of the roots. These difficulties were further compounded by imprecise notions about what numbers, in fact, are. For almost two centuries after Girard proposed his hypothesis, mathematicians had only a vague idea of the nature of complex numbers. For example, Wilhelm Gottfried Leibniz, one of the foremost mathematicians of his age, believed that there were not enough complex numbers to act as roots for all real algebraic equations. To prove his assertion he cited the equation $x^4 + 1 = 0$. This equation has the number $\sqrt{i}$, sometimes written as $\sqrt{\sqrt{-1}}$, as a solution. This number, argued Leibniz, could not be written in the form $a + bi$, where a and b are real numbers, and so by definition $\sqrt{i}$ was not a complex number. (*Complex numbers* are often defined as the set of all numbers of the form $a + bi$, where the letters a and b represent real numbers.)

We now know that Leibniz was wrong. The number $\sqrt{i}$ *is* a complex number: That is, there are real numbers a and b such that $\sqrt{i}$ can written in the form $a + bi$. It is a telling fact that the first completely rigorous proofs of the fundamental theorem of algebra were produced by the same mathematicians who also developed the first clear and rigorous way of representing complex numbers.

Further Attempts at a Proof

The first mathematician to make headway proving a very restricted version of the fundamental theorem of algebra was the Swiss mathematician and scientist Leonhard Euler (1707–93). Euler was perhaps the most prolific mathematician in history. There probably was no mathematical subject of interest in his day that he did not consider. Some authors claim that Euler, who could perform very complex calculations in his head in much the same way that Mozart is said to have composed music, was able to compose mathematical papers while playing with his grandchildren. In any case as a young man Euler published papers regularly. As he grew older he published more. He lost his eyesight 17 years before his death. One would have thought that his inability

Leonhard Euler, one of the most productive mathematicians of all time. (Library of Congress, Prints and Photographs Division)

to see and write mathematics would have slowed him down, but the rate at which he published his ideas continued to increase despite his blindness. Euler's collected works were eventually published late in the 20th century. They filled more than 80 volumes.

In the course of his research Euler found many uses for complex numbers, numbers that had previously been regarded as "imaginary" or "useless." As he learned to compute with these numbers, he learned more about their basic properties. He was able, for example, to disprove Leibniz's claim that $\sqrt{i}$ is not complex. Euler was also able to show that for any real algebraic equation of degree not greater than 6, there exist as many (possibly complex) linear factors as the degree of the equation. That is, every algebraic equation of degree n, where n is less than 7, has n roots. Euler also indicated his belief that the same sort of argument that he had discovered could be extended to equations of higher degree, but he did not undertake that project himself.

Recall that Girard's speculation applied to all equations of the form $a_n x^n + a_{n-1} x^{n-1} + \ldots + a_1 x + a_0 = 0$. He stated that for any algebraic equation of degree n there exist exactly n roots. Or equivalently, there exist n linear factors for any algebraic equation of degree n. Because n can represent any nonnegative whole number, the theorem, if true, also applies to algebraic equations of very high degree. In particular, it must apply to equations so long that we could never write them. Euler's proof was a good start. He had advanced beyond simple speculation about the theorem, but his work was far from the last word.

The French mathematicians Jean Le Rond d'Alembert (1717–83), Pierre Simon Laplace (1749–1827), and Joseph-Louis Lagrange (1736–1813) also attempted to prove the fundamental theorem of algebra. As Euler did, each of these mathematicians contributed something to the general level of understanding, and each made the truth of the fundamental theorem appear more plausible, but none produced a complete proof. By the time these very prominent mathematicians had tried their hand at proving the fundamental theorem, there were few mathematicians left who doubted the truth of the theorem.

At this point one might ask, Why bother proving the fundamental theorem when it was by this time so "obviously" true? If the fundamental theorem of algebra is almost certainly true and completing the proof is difficult, why not assume the truth and move on to the next problem? The answers to these questions lie in the nature of mathematics. Mathematics is a deductive science. Mathematicians reason from the general to the specific. Practically speaking this means that new discoveries are obtained by making logical deductions from previously established results, definitions, and axioms. In this sense mathematics is like a logical chain. Each new theorem corresponds to a new link in the chain. No new idea can be proved if the supposed proof depends on older ideas whose truth has not been firmly established.

Euler's initial goal, for example, was to prove what we now call the fundamental theorem of algebra, but this only seems to be his goal. Had he been successful in proving the statement true, he would probably have used the fundamental theorem to deduce other new results. Furthermore if he had not continued to push forward, someone else would surely have done so. No matter how difficult it might be to establish the truth of the fundamental theorem—no matter how many years of effort are invested in the proof—once it is proved, the theorem simply becomes a means to proving other newer theorems. This is mathematical progress. In the case of the fundamental theorem of algebra, mathematicians took centuries to progress from Girard's speculations to a rigorous proof.

The first person to get credit for proving the fundamental theorem of algebra was the German mathematician and scientist Carl Friedrich Gauss (1777–1855), one of the most successful mathematicians of the 19th century. Gauss showed mathematical promise at a young age and was awarded a stipend from the duke of Brunswick. The stipend made it possible for Gauss to go through high school and university and to earn a Ph.D. His "proof" of the fundamental theorem was part of his Ph.D. thesis. This was only his first proof, and there were some gaps in it, but it was a great step forward.

Gauss's proof of one of the fundamental results in mathematics did not lead him to a job immediately after graduation, however.

He did not want a job. He preferred to study, and he was able to act independently because the stipend that he received from the duke continued for several years after he was awarded the Ph.D. During this time he devoted himself to his own mathematical research. He obtained a job as director of the astronomical observatory at Göttingen University only after the duke died and his stipend was discontinued. Gauss remained in his position as director of the observatory for his entire working life.

Despite the many discoveries Gauss made throughout his life, the fundamental theorem of algebra was an especially important idea for him. As we mentioned, his first attempt at proving the fundamental theorem of algebra, the attempt that earned him a Ph.D., had several gaps in it. He later revised the proof to correct its initial deficiencies. In fact Gauss never stopped tinkering with the fundamental theorem of algebra. He later published a third proof, and when he wanted to celebrate the 50th anniversary of receiving his Ph.D., he published a fourth proof. Each proof approached the problem from a slightly different perspective. He died not long after his fourth proof, his mathematical career bracketed by the fundamental theorem of algebra.

Gauss's eventual success in developing a completely rigorous proof of the fundamental theorem was due, in part, to his firm grasp of the nature of complex numbers. It is no coincidence that he was also one of the first mathematicians to develop a clear, geometrical interpretation of the complex number system. Gauss represented the complex number system as points on a plane. Each complex number $a + bi$ is interpreted as a point (a, b) in the so-called complex plane (see the accompanying figure, on page 87). This geometric representation of the complex number system is the one that is in common use today. Gauss was not the only person to have this particular insight. Though the idea seems simple enough, it was a very important innovation. This is demonstrated by the fact that after centuries of work, two of the earliest individuals to discover this clear and unambiguous interpretation of the complex number system also discovered proofs of the fundamental theorem of algebra.

Another early proof of the fundamental theorem of algebra was given by Jean Robert Argand (1768–1822). Argand was Swiss-born. He was a quiet, unassuming man. Little is known of his early background or even of his education. We do know that he lived in Paris and worked as a bookkeeper and accountant, that he was married and had children, and that as much as he enjoyed the study of mathematics, it was for him just a hobby.

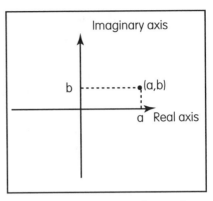

The complex number a + bi *can be represented as a point on a plane.*

Argand was not especially aggressive in making himself known to other mathematicians. In 1806 he published a thin mathematics book at his own expense. In it one finds two of the most important ideas of the time: a geometrical representation of the complex numbers and a proof of the fundamental theorem of algebra. Because the book was published anonymously, years later, when the work had finally attracted the attention of some of the best mathematicians of the day, a call went out for the unknown author to identify himself and claim credit for the ideas contained in the work. It was only then that Argand stepped forward to identify himself as the author. He later published a small number of additional papers that commented on the work of other authors or elaborated on the work contained in his original, anonymously published book.

Argand's geometric representation of the complex numbers is today known as the Argand diagram. It is the interpretation of the complex numbers that students learn first when introduced to the subject. His proof that every algebraic equation of degree n with complex coefficients has n roots would also seem familiar to students interested in more advanced algebra. His approach to proving the fundamental theorem is similar to a common modern proof.

The proofs of Cauchy and Argand were just the first few in a long line of different proofs of the fundamental theorem of algebra. As mathematicians' understanding of complex numbers and the functions that depend on them deepened, they developed a branch of mathematics called the theory of complex variables. This, essentially, is calculus using complex—as opposed to real—numbers. Here again the fundamental theorem of algebra plays an important role, and an entirely new proof of the theorem—this time using ideas from the theory of complex variables—was

USING POLYNOMIALS

For much of the history of the human race, mathematicians have worked to understand the mathematical structure of polynomials. They have developed algorithms to find the roots of polynomials, they have developed algorithms that allow them to approximate the roots of polynomials, and they have studied the mathematical relationships that exist between algebraic (polynomial) equations and their roots. The study of polynomials has occupied some of the best mathematical minds throughout much of the history of humanity, but none of this work provides an immediate answer to the question, What are polynomials good for?

Polynomials play an important role in scientific and engineering computations. In many

Polynomials play an essential role in applied mathematics. This simulation of the temperature profile of air in the wake of a speeding bullet was developed at the National Institute for Standards and Technology, one of the leading research institutes in the United States. (Courtesy Pedro Espina/National Institute of Standards and Technology)

discovered. Each new proof establishes new connections between the fundamental theorem and other branches of mathematics.

The fundamental theorem of algebra is the culmination of a theory of equations that began with the work of ancient Mesopotamian scribes pressing triangular shapes into slabs of wet clay on the hot plains of Mesopotamia thousands of years ago. It illuminates basic connections between polynomials and the complex number system. It does not solve every problem associated with polynomials, of course. There were still questions, for exam-

of the mathematical equations that arise in these disciplines, the unknown is not a number but a function. That function may represent the path of a rocket through space or, in meteorology, the position of a high-pressure front as it moves across Earth's surface. Equations that have functions, instead of numbers, for solutions are often exceedingly difficult to solve. In fact, as a general rule, the precise solutions are often impossible to calculate. The strategy that applied scientists adopt, therefore, is to construct a function that approximates the exact solution. A polynomial, or a set of polynomials, is often the ideal choice for an approximating solution. There are two main reasons polynomials are so widely used.

First, polynomials are well-understood mathematical functions. In addition to the fundamental theorem of algebra there are a host of other theorems that describe their mathematical properties. These theorems enable scientists and engineers to calculate with polynomials with relative ease.

Second, there are many polynomials to choose from. This means that in many problems of practical importance there are sufficiently many polynomials to enable the scientist or engineer to calculate a very accurate approximation to the solution by using only polynomials. This method is often used despite the fact that the exact solution to the equation in which they have an interest is not a polynomial at all.

These two facts have been known to mathematicians since the 19th century, but the computational difficulties involved in calculating the desired polynomials often made applying these ideas too difficult. With the advent of computers, however, many of the computational difficulties disappeared, so that from a practical point of view polynomials are now more important than ever.

ple, about the computational techniques needed to approximate the roots of polynomials and about the role of polynomials in broader classes of functions. Furthermore special classes of polynomials would eventually be identified for their utility in solving practical computational problems in science and engineering. (This research would be further accelerated by the invention of computers.) And, finally, the fundamental theorem itself sheds no light on why the methods that had proved so useful for finding the roots of algebraic equations of degree less than 5 would, in general, prove ineffective for finding the roots of equations of degree 5 or more. Nevertheless the fundamental theorem shows how several properties of polynomials that had been of interest to mathematicians for the last 4,000 years are related.

- It relates the degree of an equation to the number of its solutions.

- It demonstrates that, in theory, any polynomial can be factored.

- It shows that the complex number system contains all solutions to the set of all algebraic equations.

Research into algebra did not end with the fundamental theorem of algebra, of course; it shifted focus from the study of the solutions of polynomials toward a more general study of the logical structure of mathematical systems.

5

ALGEBRA IN GEOMETRY
AND ANALYSIS

In the 17th century mathematicians began to express geometric relationships algebraically. Algebraic descriptions are in many ways preferable to the geometric descriptions favored by the ancient Greeks. They are often more concise and usually easier to manipulate. But to obtain these descriptions, mathematicians needed a way of connecting the geometric ideas of lines, curves, and surfaces with algebraic symbols. The discovery of a method for effecting this connection—now called analytic geometry—had a profound impact on the history of mathematics and on the history of science in general. The ideas mathematicians developed in the process have become so ingrained in modern approaches to mathematics that today many students acquire their mathematical education without ever encountering another way of understanding mathematics.

To be fair, not all the ideas presently credited to these 17th-century mathematicians originated with them. Some of the more important ideas in analytic geometry are present in the work of the ancient Greeks. The Greek mathematician Menaechmus (ca. 380 B.C.E.–ca. 320 B.C.E.) is sometimes credited with discovering how to express geometric relationships algebraically. Unfortunately none of his work survived to modern times. We know of him only through the descriptions of his work found in the writings of others. From these descriptions we know that Menaechmus was concerned with geometric relations that *we* would express in terms of equations such as $a/x = x/y$ and $x/y = y/b$. If, for example, we were to multiply both sides of the first of these equations by xy, we would obtain the equation $ay = x^2$, an equation that students everywhere now learn to associate with the graph of a parabola. Menaechmus was certainly familiar with parabolas. Some authors think he may have coined the term, but he probably did not understand a parabola as the set of all points in the plane that satisfy this or some similar equation.

As other Greek mathematicians did, Menaechmus conceived of a parabola as the set of all points belonging to the intersection of a plane and a cone, when the plane takes a certain orientation relative to the cone (see the accompanying figure). Whatever his contributions may have been in this regard—however close he was to an algebraic description of a parabola or other curve—he almost certainly did not make the jump from geometric to algebraic language. The Greeks of Menaechmus's time did not know elementary algebra in the sense that we now understand the term.

The Greek mathematician Apollonius of Perga (ca. 262 B.C.E.–ca. 190 B.C.E.), another mathematician who is sometimes credited with coining the terms *parabola*, *hyperbola*, and *ellipse*, also was close to making an important connection between algebra and geometry. Apollonius was one of the most thoughtful and prolific of all the ancient Greek mathematicians. His most famous work is *Conics*, most of which has survived. As the name implies, the topic with which Apollonius concerns himself in his great work is the

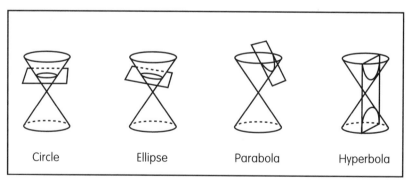

Circle   Ellipse   Parabola   Hyperbola

The Greeks described the parabola as the intersection of a cone and a plane when the plane is parallel to a line generating the cone.

mathematical properties of conic sections. (The *conic sections* are ellipses, hyperbolas, and parabolas.) In his study of conic sections Apollonius develops a way of imposing a coordinate system on his diagram.

A *planar coordinate system* is a correspondence between ordered pairs of numbers and points on the plane. Given a point on the plane, the coordinate system enables the user to associate an ordered pair of numbers, and given an ordered pair of numbers, the coordinate system enables the user to associate with them a point on the plane. Today as a result of long familiarity, the concept seems to be an easy one. It is used in board games that depend on a grid system and maps that use longitude and latitude or a similar method to establish position. The idea may seem almost trivial, but its usefulness cannot be overstated. The development of coordinate systems has made a huge difference in the development of both science and mathematics.

The coordinate system devised by Apollonius was not the kind of coordinate system with which most of us are familiar today. His axes, for example, were generally not perpendicular to one another. Nonperpendicular axes—often called oblique axes—are awkward to use when one wants to calculate distances between points, for example, but they are perfectly adequate for establishing the necessary correspondence between pairs of numbers and points on the plane.

Another important difference between Apollonius's use of a coordinate system and our modern approach is that Apollonius established the conic section first and constructed the coordinate system later—that is, if he constructed one at all. Today, of course, we often begin with a coordinate system and then graph the curve of interest—conic section or otherwise—onto the preassigned coordinate system. (We do this so often that many of us never learn another way of representing curves, but there are other ways. Coordinate systems are tremendously important, but they are not the only technique available.)

Despite the differences between Apollonius's use of coordinates and our more modern approaches, Apollonius's insights into the use of coordinates were very penetrating. He recognized something of their importance, and he evidently understood how to change from one coordinate system to another. Changing from one system to another is important because it is always the curve or surface under study, not the coordinate system, in which the mathematician has an interest. The coordinate system is just a tool to facilitate that study. There is no one "right" coordinate system; in fact, there is a lot of arbitrariness in how one chooses a coordinate system. Furthermore, the answers that a mathematician obtains through the use of a coordinate system are expressed in terms of a particular system of coordinates.

Two mathematicians studying the same object may choose different coordinate systems, and so their final results may well look different. Are these differences important or are they just artifacts of the coordinate systems that the mathematicians chose? To answer this question it is necessary to develop a procedure to switch from one coordinate system to another. Apollonius knew how to do this. In this sense, too, he was very modern. Despite all of his creativity and mathematical ingenuity, however, Apollonius's insights into the value of coordinate systems had little effect on those who followed him.

One reason that Apollonius's insights into coordinate systems did not have more impact on the development of mathematics was that the Greeks had little interest in algebra. The Greek mathematical tradition continued for about eight centuries, and for most of that time they studied no algebra. Diophantus was the exception, but he lived toward the end of the age of Greek mathematics. In any case, the very concise, abstract language of algebra was unknown to any ancient Greek mathematician. Throughout the 800 years that the Greeks studied geometry, they communicated their ideas through diagrams and long, often complicated prose. The curves that they did study were described in this very cumbersome way; probably their cumbersomeness helps to account for the fact that they studied very few curves. In fact all told for 800 years the Greeks restricted their research to about a dozen or so curves. They did not need a general technique for the description of curves because they confined their attention to a small number of special cases.

All of this had changed by the beginning of the 17th century. By then many of the most important mathematical works of ancient Greece had been rediscovered. The beautiful but very taxing diagrams that Apollonius and others had used to describe their insights had become well known to many European mathematicians. Algebra had flourished in the interim, and the innovations of François Viète and others had prepared the ground for a hybridization of algebraic and geometric ideas and techniques. To be sure Viète's algebraic language was not the one we use today, but its usefulness was already apparent. The great innovation was to draw together what had been two very separate disciplines, algebra and geometry, and to use ideas in each to solve problems in the other. The opportunity to do this was seized independently and almost simultaneously by two mathematicians, René Descartes and Pierre de Fermat.

René Descartes

The French mathematician, scientist, and philosopher René Descartes (1596–1650) was one of the more colorful characters in the history of mathematics. Although we will concentrate on his ideas about mathematics, his contributions to several branches of science are just as important as his mathematical innovations, and today he is perhaps best remembered as a philosopher.

Descartes was born into comfortable surroundings. Although his mother died when he was an infant, his father, a lawyer, ensured that Descartes received an excellent education. As a youth Descartes displayed a quick

René Descartes, philosopher, scientist, and mathematician. (Topham/The Image Works)

intellect, and he was described by those who knew him at the time as a boy with an endless series of questions. He attended the Royal College at La Flèche and the University of Poitiers, but the more education he received, the less pleasure he seemed to derive from it. Given his academic record this is a little surprising. He was a talented writer who demonstrated a real gift for learning languages. He also displayed an early interest in science and math. The Royal College, where he received his early education, accommodated his idiosyncrasies: The rector at the school allowed Descartes to spend his mornings in bed. Descartes enjoyed lying in bed thinking, and he apparently maintained this habit for most of his life. Nevertheless by the time he graduated from college he was confused and disappointed. He felt that he had learned little of which he could be sure. It was a deficiency that he spent a lifetime correcting.

After college Descartes wandered across Europe for a number of years. On occasion he enlisted in an army. This was not an uncommon way for a young gentleman to pass the time. He claimed that as a young man he enjoyed war, though there are conflicting opinions about how much time he spent fighting and how much time he spent "lying in" each morning. (Ideas about military discipline have changed in the intervening centuries.) In addition to his military adventures, Descartes took the time to meet intellectuals and to exchange ideas. This went on for about a decade. Eventually, however, he settled in Holland, where he remained for almost two decades, writing and thinking.

Holland was a good place for Descartes. His ideas were new and radical, and like most radical ideas, good and bad, Descartes's ideas were not especially popular. In a less tolerant country, he would have been in great danger, but because he was under the protection of the Dutch leader, the prince of Orange, he was safe from physical harm. Though he was not physically attacked for his ideas, there was a period when his books were banned.

During his stay in Holland Descartes applied himself to exploring and describing his ideas in mathematics, science, and philosophy. In mathematics his major discoveries can be found in the book *Discours de la méthode* (Discourse on method), especially in an appendix to this work that described his ideas on geometry. It is in the *Discours* that Descartes makes the necessary connections between geometry and algebra that resulted in a new branch of mathematics. It is also in this book that he developed most of the algebraic symbolism that we use today. With very few exceptions, Descartes's algebra resembles our algebra. (The reason is that our algebra is modeled on Descartes's.) Most modern readers can understand Descartes's own equations without difficulty.

One of Descartes's simpler and yet very important contributions was to reinterpret ideas that were already known. Since the days of the ancient Greeks, an unknown was associated with a line segment. If we call the unknown x, the product of x with itself was interpreted as a square. This is why we call the symbol x^2 "x squared." This geometric interpretation had been a great conceptual aid to the Greeks, but over the intervening centuries it had become a barrier to progress. The difficulty was not with x^2 or even $x \times x \times x$, written x^3 and called "x cubed." The symbol x^3 was interpreted as a three-dimensional cube. The problem with this geometric interpretation was that it required one to imagine a four-dimensional "cube" for the product of x with itself four times, a five-dimensional cube for the product of x with itself five times, and so forth. This impeded understanding. The great mathematician Omar Khayyám, for example, was unable to assign a meaning to a polynomial of degree 4, because he was not able to see past this type of geometric interpretation of the symbol x^4.

Descartes still imagined the variable x as representing a line segment of indeterminate length. His innovation was the way he imagined higher powers of x and, more generally, the geometric interpretation he gave products. Descartes, for example, simply imagined x, x^2, x^3, x^4, and so forth, as representing a line segment, and products of two different variables, x and y, as representing the length of a third line segment of length xy instead of a rectangle of area xy as the Greeks and their successors had imagined. To make the idea palatable, he described it geometrically (see the sidebar Descartes on Multiplication).

Descartes's contributions to modern analytic geometry are extremely important, but his understanding of the subject was

DESCARTES ON MULTIPLICATION

In more modern terminology, the Greeks established a correspondence between the length of line segments and what we would call real numbers. A number of magnitude *x* would be represented by a segment of length *x*. The product of two numbers *x* and *y* was represented as a rectangle with the segment of length *x* forming one side of the rectangle and the segment of length *y* forming the other. This

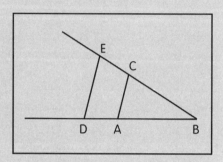

Descartes's geometric interpretation of the operation of multiplication.

works well until one wants to consider products of numbers *u, v, x,* and *y.* Most of us have a difficult time picturing a way of orienting line segments of length *u, v, x,* and *y* so as to form a four-dimensional rectangular solid.

Descartes's innovation was to use triangles rather than rectangles and imagine all products as simply line segments of the appropriate length. We use the accompanying diagram to paraphrase Descartes's ideas on multiplication. If we imagine

still profoundly different from ours. We acknowledge his contribution by calling the most common of all coordinate systems in use today the Cartesian coordinate system, but Descartes made little use of Cartesian coordinates. To be sure, he recognized the value of coordinates as a tool in bridging the subjects of algebra and geometry, but, as Apollonius did, he generally used oblique coordinates. Furthermore because he questioned the reality of negative numbers, he refrained from using negative coordinates. As a consequence Descartes restricted himself to what we would call the first quadrant, that part of the coordinate plane where both coordinates are positive. He did, however, recognize and exploit the connection between equations and geometric curves, and this was extremely important.

- the distance from *A* to *B* as one unit long

- the distance from *A* to *C* as *x* units long and

- the distance from *B* to *D* as *y* units long

then we can construct a segment passing through *D* that is parallel to the line *AC*. Segment *DE* is this parallel line segment. The triangles *ABC* and *DBE* are similar, so the ratios of their corresponding sides are equal. In symbols this is written as

$$AC/1 = DE/BD$$

or using *x* and *y* in place of *AC* and *AD*, respectively,

$$x/1 = DE/y$$

or, finally, solving for *DE*, we get

$$xy = DE$$

With this diagram Descartes provided a new and more productive geometric interpretation of arithmetic.

Descartes's innovation freed mathematicians from the limiting ideas of Greek and Islamic mathematicians about the meaning of multiplication and other arithmetic operations. He also showed that the requirement of homogeneity that had made using Viète's algebra so awkward was unnecessary.

In Descartes's time conic sections—ellipses, parabolas, and hyperbolas—were still generally described geometrically. Descartes explored the connections between the geometric description of conic sections and algebraic equations. He did this by examining the connections between geometry and the *algebraic* equation $y^2 = ay - bxy + cx - dx^2 + e$. (In this equation *x* and *y* are the variables and *a*, *b*, *c*, *d*, and *e* are the coefficients.) Depending on how one chooses the coefficients one can obtain an algebraic description of any of the conic sections. For example, if *a*, *b*, and *c* are chosen to be 0 and *d* and *e* are positive, then the equation describes an ellipse. If, on the other hand, *a*, *b*, *d*, and *e* are taken as 0 and *c* is not 0 then the graph is a parabola. Descartes went much further in exploring the connections between algebra and geometry than any of his predecessors, and in doing so he demonstrated how mathematically powerful these ideas are.

What, in retrospect, may have been Descartes's most important discoveries received much less attention from their discoverer than they deserved. Descartes recognized that when one equation

---

448   ŒUVRES DE DESCARTES.   375.

Que fi on veut, au contraire, diminuer de trois la raçine de cete mefme Equation, il faut faire

$$y + 3 \infty x \quad \& \quad yy + 6y + 9 \infty xx,$$

& ainfi des autres. De façon qu'au lieu de

$$x^4 + 4x^3 - 19xx - 106x - 120 \infty 0, \qquad 5$$

on met

$$y^4 + 12y^3 + 54yy + 108y + 81$$
$$+ \ 4y^3 + 36yy + 108y + 108$$
$$- 19yy - 114y - 171$$
$$- 106y - 318 \qquad 10$$
$$- 120$$

$$\overline{y^4 + 16y^3 + 71yy - \ 4y - 420 \infty 0.}$$

Qu'en augmentant les vrayes racines, on diminue les fauffes, & au contraire. Et il eft a remarquer qu'en diminuant les vrayes racines d'vne Equation, on diminue les fauffes de la mefme quantité, ou, au contraire, en diminuant les 15 vrayes, on augmente les fauffes; & que, fi on diminue, foit les vnes, foit les autres, d'vne quantité qui leur foit efgale, elles deuienent nulles, & que, fi c'eft d'vne quantité qui les furpaffe, de vrayes elles deuienent fauffes, ou de fauffes, vrayes. Comme icy, 20 en augmentant de 3 la vraye racine, qui eftoit 5, on a diminué de 3 chafcune des fauffes, en forte que celle qui eftoit 4 n'eft plus qu'1, & celle qui eftoit 3 eft nulle, & que celle qui eftoit 2 eft deuenue vraye & eft 1, a caufe que − 2 + 3 fait + 1. C'eft pourquoy, en cete 25 Equation,

$$y^3 - 8yy - 1y + 8 \infty 0,$$

il n'y a plus que 3 racines, entre lefquelles il y en a

A page from Descartes's Discours *showing how similar Descartes's algebraic notation is to modern notation.* (Courtesy of University of Vermont) contains two unknowns, which we call x and y, there is generally more than one solution to the equation. In other words, given a value for x, we can, under fairly general conditions, find a value for y such that together the two numbers satisfy the one equation. The set of all such solutions as x varies over some interval forms a curve. These observations can be made mathematically precise, and the precise expression of these ideas is often called the fundamental principle of analytic geometry. Descartes knew the fundamental principle of analytic geometry, but he seems to have considered it less important than some of the other ideas contained in his work.

The fundamental principle of analytic geometry is important because it freed mathematicians from the paucity of curves that had been familiar to the ancient Greeks. Here was a method for generating infinitely many new curves: Simply write one equation in two variables; the result, subject to a few not-very-demanding conditions, is another new curve. Descartes went even further. A single equation that involves exactly three variables—x, y, and z, for example—in general, describes a surface. This is called the fundamental principle of solid analytic geometry, and it, too, was known to Descartes. Today this is recognized as a very important idea, but its importance does not seem to have been recognized by Descartes. He gives a clear statement of the principle but does not follow it with either examples or further discussion. He understood the idea, but he did not use it.

The principles of analytic and solid geometry, so clearly enunciated by Descartes, were important because they pointed to a way of greatly enriching the vocabulary of mathematics. Conic sections and a handful of other curves, as well as cylinders, spheres, and some other surfaces, had been studied intensively for millennia, in part because few other curves and solids had convenient mathematical descriptions. Descartes's insights had made these restrictions a thing of the past. He was aware of this; it had been one of his goals: He wrote that he wanted to free mathematics from the difficult diagrams of the ancients, and in this regard he was successful. His algebra and the fundamental principles of analytic geometry and solid geometry were his most insightful discoveries in this sense.

Descartes's discoveries in science, mathematics, and philosophy eventually attracted the attention of the queen of Sweden. Queen Christina invited him to become a member of her court, and Descartes accepted. Descartes was not a man who liked the cold. Nor did he like to get up early in the morning. (He had maintained his habit of spending his mornings in bed throughout his life.) On his arrival in September Descartes must have been dismayed to learn that Queen Christina, on the other hand, liked to receive her instruction from her new philosopher at five in the morning. Descartes died in the cold of a Swedish December, less than five months after arriving at the queen's court.

Pierre de Fermat

The French mathematician and lawyer Pierre de Fermat (1601–65) also discovered analytic geometry, and he did so independently of René Descartes. Little is known of Fermat's early life. He was educated as a lawyer, and it was in the field of law that he spent his working life. He worked in the local parliament in Toulouse, France, and later he worked in the criminal court. We also know that he had an unusual facility with languages. He spoke several languages and enjoyed reading classical literature. He is best remembered for his contributions to mathematics, which were profound.

Today much of what we know of Fermat is derived from the numerous letters that he wrote. He maintained an active correspondence with many of the leading mathematicians of his time. His letters show him to be humble, polite, and extremely curious. He made important contributions to the development of probability theory, the theory of numbers, and some aspects of calculus, as well as analytic geometry. Mathematics was, however, only one of his hobbies.

One activity that Fermat shared with many of the mathematicians of his time was the "reconstruction" of lost ancient texts. By the early 17th century some of the works of the ancient Greek mathematicians had again become available. These were, for the most part, the same texts with which we are familiar today. Most of the ancient texts, however, had been lost in the intervening centuries. Although the works had been lost, they had not been forgotten. The lost works were often known through commentaries written by other ancient mathematicians. The ancient commentaries described the work of other mathematicians, but often they were much more than simple descriptions. Sometimes a commentary contained corrections, suggestions, or alternative proofs of known results; on occasion, the commentaries even contained entirely new theorems that extended those appearing in the work that was the subject of the commentary. Other times, however, a commentary simply mentioned the title of a work in passing. In any case, much of what we know about Greek mathematics and Greek mathematicians we know through the commentaries. It had become fashionable among mathematicians of the 17th century to try to reconstruct lost works on the basis of information gained from these secondary sources. Fermat attempted to reconstruct the book *Plane Loci* by Apollonius on the basis of information contained in a commentary written by the Greek geometer Pappus of Alexandria.

Some of Apollonius's most important work, once thought lost, was rediscovered in the 20th century in an ancient Arabic translation, but the book *Plane Loci* seems to have been permanently lost. We will never know how close Fermat was in his reconstruction to the original, but the effort was not wasted. While attempting the reconstruction Fermat discovered the fundamental principle of analytic geometry: Under very general conditions, a single equation in two variables describes a curve in the plane.

As Descartes did, Fermat worked hard to establish algebraic descriptions of conic sections. Hyperbolas, ellipses, and parabolas were, after all, the classic curves of antiquity, and any attempt to express geometry in the language of algebra had at least to take these curves into account in order to be successful. Fermat was extremely thorough in his analysis. Again as Descartes did, he analyzed a very general second-degree equation in the variables x and y. Fermat's method was to manipulate the equation until he had reduced it to one of several standard equations. Each *standard equation* represented a class of equations that were similar in the sense that each equation in the class could be transformed into another equation via one or more elementary operations. (The standard equation that he obtained depended on the initial values of the coefficients.) Finally, Fermat showed that each of these standard equations described the intersection of a plane with Apollonius's cone. He had found a correspondence between a class of curves and a class of equations. This analysis was an important illustration of the utility of the new methods.

As Descartes did, Fermat used coordinates as a way of bridging the separate disciplines of algebra and geometry. Fermat, too, was comfortable using oblique coordinates as well as what we now call Cartesian coordinates.

As might be expected, Fermat and Descartes were each well aware of the work of the other. They even corresponded with each other through the French priest and mathematician Marin Mersenne (1588–1648). Mersenne was a friend of both men and a talented mathematician in his own right. In addition he opened his home to weekly meetings of mathematicians in the Paris area and worked hard to spread the news about discoveries in mathematics and the sciences throughout Europe.

Despite the many similarities in their work on analytic geometry and the fact that they both made their discoveries known to Mersenne, Descartes had much more influence on the development of the subject than did Fermat. One reason was that Fermat did not publish very much. In fact, Fermat only published a single paper during his lifetime. It was only later that his writings were collected and made generally available. Moreover, unlike Descartes, who had a flair for good algebraic notation, Fermat used the older, more awkward notation of François Viète.

Surprisingly despite his importance to the subject, Fermat's principal mathematical interest was number theory, not analytic geometry. Although he tried to interest others in problems in the theory of numbers, Fermat was largely unsuccessful. For the most part, he worked on his favorite subject alone. His isolation, however, seemed to pose no barrier to creative thinking. He discovered a number of important results as well as a famous conjecture called Fermat's last theorem (see the sidebar).

FERMAT'S LAST THEOREM

One of Fermat's most famous insights is his so-called last theorem. This problem, which was finally solved late in the 20th century, is one of the most famous problems in the history of mathematics. It can, however, be understood as a generalization of a much older problem, the problem of finding Pythagorean triples. (The clay tablet called Plimpton 322–a photograph of which appears in chapter 1–contains a list of Pythagorean triples in cuneiform.) A Pythagorean triple is a set of three natural numbers with the property that if each number of the triple is squared then the sum of the two smaller squares equals

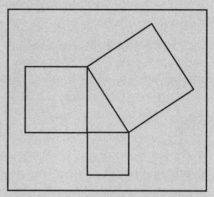

The sum of the areas of the two smaller squares equals the area of the largest square. The lengths of the sides of the triangle on which the squares are constructed are in the ratio 3:4:5.

the largest square. For example, the set (3, 4, 5) is a Pythagorean triple because, first, each number in the triple is a natural number, and, second, the three numbers satisfy the equation $x^2 + y^2 = z^2$, where we can let x, y, and z represent 3, 4, and 5, respectively. Another way of understanding the same problem is that we have represented the number 25, which is a perfect square, as the sum of two smaller perfect squares, 9 and 16. There are infinitely many Pythagorean triples, a fact of which the Mesopotamians seemed fully aware. (The Mesopotamians' work on Pythagorean triples is discussed in chapter 1.)

The generalization of the Pythagorean theorem of interest to Fermat involved writing natural numbers greater than 2 in place of the exponent in the equation $x^2 + y^2 = z^2$. The resulting equation is $x^n + y^n = z^n$, where n belongs to the set (3, 4, 5, . . .). When n is equal to 3 we can interpret the problem geometrically: We are searching for three cubes, each of which has an edge that is an integral number of units long, such that the volume of the largest cube equals the sum of the two smaller volumes. When n is greater than 3 we can describe the problem in terms of hyper-

(continues)

FERMAT'S LAST THEOREM
(continued)

cubes, but in higher dimensions there is no easy-to-visualize generalization of the two- and three-dimensional interpretations described earlier.

Fermat's goal, then, was to find a triplet of natural numbers that satisfies any one of the following equations $x^3 + y^3 = z^3$, $x^4 + y^4 = z^4$, $x^5 + y^5 = z^5$, . . . He was unable to find a single solution for any exponent larger than 2. In fact, he wrote that he had found a wonderful proof that *there were no solutions* for any n larger than 2, but the margin of the book in which he was writing was too small to contain the proof of this discovery. No trace of Fermat's proof has ever been discovered, but his cryptic note inspired generations of mathematicians, amateur and professional, to try to develop their own proofs. Before World War I a large monetary prize was offered, and this inspired many more faulty proofs.

Throughout most of the 20th century mathematicians proved that solutions did not exist for various special cases. For example, it was eventually proved that if a solution did exist for a particular value of n, then n had to be larger than 25,000. *Most* integers, however, are larger than 25,000, so this type of result hardly scratches the surface. In the late 20th century, Fermat's theorem was finally proved by using mathematics that would have been entirely unfamiliar to Fermat. The British-born mathematician Andrew Wiles devised the proof, which is about 150 pages long.

Wiles and many others do not believe that Fermat actually had a proof. They think that the proof that Fermat thought he had discovered actually had an error in it. This kind of thing is not uncommon in a difficult logical argument; Wiles himself initially published an incorrect proof of Fermat's theorem. Nevertheless, unlike most of his successors, Fermat was an epoch-making mathematician. As a consequence it would be wrong to discount completely the possibility that he had found a valid proof using only mathematics from the 17th century, but at present it does not seem likely.

The New Approach

Descartes and Fermat developed a new symbolic language that enabled them to bridge the gap that had separated algebra from geometry. This language contributed to progress in both fields. They had learned to connect the formerly separate disciplines of algebra and geometry: Algebraic operations represented the manipulation of geometric objects, and geometric manipulations could now be expressed in a compact, algebraic form. Descartes and Fermat had made an important conceptual breakthrough, and unlike many other new mathematical ideas, these ideas were immediately recognized by their contemporaries as valuable.

Mathematicians interested in geometry exploited the fundamental principles of analytic and solid geometry to develop new ways of describing old curves and surfaces. They also developed entirely new curves and surfaces. The exploration of geometry from an algebraic point of view and the application of geometry to algebra challenged many fine mathematicians. Descartes and Fermat had opened up a new mathematical landscape, and for several generations thereafter, mathematicians worked to extend the ideas and techniques that Descartes and Fermat had pioneered. It would be a long time before progress in analytic geometry began to slow.

The geometric interpretation of algebraic quantities also influenced other branches of mathematics and science. Perhaps most importantly, the language of analytic geometry, somewhat modified and augmented, became the language of analysis, that branch of mathematics that arose out of calculus. Calculus was discovered twice, once by the British physicist and mathematician Sir Isaac Newton (1643–1727), and again independently by the German philosopher, mathematician, and diplomat Gottfried Wilhelm Leibniz (1646–1716).

The new analysis enabled the user to solve problems in geometry and physics that had previously been too difficult. In fact, early in the development of analysis certain problems in geometry that Descartes himself had believed to be unsolvable were solved. The techniques the analysts used often required a great deal of analytic geometry. Newton, for example, invented and employed a number of coordinate systems to facilitate his study of both physics and geometry. Some of these coordinate systems have proved to be more important than others, but in every case they were extensions of the concepts of Descartes and Fermat: Each coordinate system established a correspondence between ordered sets of real numbers and geometric points. Each coordinate system served as a bridge between the magnitudes of geometry—those continually varying quantities, such as length, area, and volume—and the numbers and symbols of algebra.

Newton generally interpreted the variables that arose in his studies as representing geometric magnitudes. In his studies of physics, however, Newton sometimes interpreted variables as magnitudes of another sort: forces, accelerations, and velocities. We take symbolic notation for granted today, but the symbolic language developed by some of these mathematicians contributed substantially to progress in the mathematical and physical sciences. Newton's notation was, however, only a modest extension of the notation used in the analytic geometry of his time. Newton absorbed the ideas of Descartes and Fermat and used these ideas throughout his work. He managed to develop a new branch of mathematics that used their notation, but he did not contribute much new notation himself.

Leibniz, who was much more gifted in languages than was Newton, greatly extended the notation of Descartes and Fermat to create a highly expressive symbolic language that was ideally suited to the new mathematics. He used this notation to express the ideas of analysis in a much more sophisticated way than that of Newton. He, too, generally interpreted the symbols that arose in his study of calculus as geometric or physical magnitudes. It was one of Leibniz's great accomplishments to extend the language of analytic geometry until it fit the problems in which he had an interest.

The role of good notation is sometimes expressed by saying that with good notation the pencil becomes as smart as the holder. To see the difference that good algebraic notation makes, knowing something about the early history of calculus is helpful. British mathematicians were more heavily influenced by Newton than they were by Leibniz. They considered it a matter of national honor to use the notation of their countryman. Unfortunately for them, Newton's notation was not expressive enough to be especially useful. In continental Europe, however, mathematicians wholeheartedly adopted Leibniz's notation, which was far superior to that of Newton. Leibniz devised his symbols to embody several basic concepts of calculus in order to communicate his ideas more effectively. This system facilitated discovery both for him and for those who followed. As a consequence calculus initially evolved much more slowly on the British Isles than it did on the Continent.

Today Leibniz's notation is still used in analysis, and the interpretation of algebraic symbols as geometric magnitudes or as physical magnitudes is still one of the basic conceptual approaches of the geometer and the analyst. So thoroughly have algebraic notation and language pervaded geometry and analysis that whether mathematicians who specialize in these subjects could express their discoveries without the use of them is doubtful. But this was just the beginning. Algebra changed radically more than once in the years following the revolution of Descartes and Fermat.

6

THE SEARCH FOR NEW
STRUCTURES

Early in the 19th century the nature of algebra changed again. Extraordinary new ideas were introduced. They changed the nature of every branch of mathematics that depends on algebra— and today *every* branch of mathematics depends on algebra. They caused mathematicians to perceive their subject in new ways, and this new perspective enabled them to imagine and solve entirely new kinds of problems.

When the new algebra was first introduced, its importance was not generally recognized. Some of the first groundbreaking papers were dismissed because the reviewers, who were among the best mathematicians of their day, did not understand the ideas involved. To those responsible for the innovations, however- er, the power of the new ideas and techniques was apparent. Some of the first applications of the new algebra involved solv- ing some of the oldest, most intractable problems in the history of mathematics. For example, the new algebra enabled mathe- maticians to prove that the three classic problems of antiquity, the squaring of the circle, the trisection of the angle, and the doubling of the cube (all performed with a straightedge and compass) are unsolvable. In addition, they showed that the problem of finding an algorithm for factoring any fifth-degree polynomial—an algorithm similar in spirit to the one that Tartaglia discovered in the 16th century for factoring a third- degree polynomial—could not be solved because the algorithm does not exist.

These very important dis-
coveries were made under
very difficult conditions. We
often forget how important
disease and violence were in
shaping much of the history
of Europe. Their role is
revealed in their effects on
the lives of these highly creative mathematicians. These
young people lived short,
hard, often miserable lives.
They faced one difficulty
after another as best they
could, and they never
stopped creating mathematics. On the night before he
expected to die, the central
figure in this mathematical
drama, a young mathemati-
cian named Évariste Galois,
spent his time hurriedly writing down as much of what he
had learned about mathematics as possible so that his
insights, which were wholly
unrecognized during his brief life, would not be lost.

*Since the work of Niels Abel and
Évariste Galois, many algebraists
have been occupied with the discovery
and exploitation of mathematical
structures of ever-increasing
sophistication.* (Library of Congress,
Prints and Photographs Division)

Broadly speaking the mathematical revolution that occurred in
algebra early in the 19th century was a move away from computation and toward the identification and exploitation of the structur-
al underpinnings of mathematics. Underlying any mathematical
system is a kind of logical structure. Often the structure is not
immediately apparent, but research into these structures has generally proved to be the most direct way of understanding the
mathematical system itself. About 200 years ago mathematicians
began to identify and use some of these structures, and they have
been busy extending their insights ever since.

Niels Henrik Abel

The Norwegian mathematician Niels Henrik Abel (1802–29) was one of the first and most important of the new mathematicians. As many 17th-, 18th-, and 19th-century mathematicians were, he was the son of a minister. The elder Abel was also a political activist, and he tutored Niels at home until the boy was 13 years old. Niels Abel attended secondary school in Christiania, now called Oslo. While there, he had the good fortune to have a mathematics teacher named Bernt Holmboe, who recognized his talent and worked with him to develop it. Under Holmboe's guidance Abel studied the works of earlier generations of mathematicians, such as Leonhard Euler, as well as the mathematical discoveries of his contemporaries, such as Carl Friedrich Gauss. In addition to exposing Abel to some of the most important works in mathematics, Holmboe also suggested original problems for Abel to solve. Abel's ability to do mathematics even at this young age was stunning.

Abel's father died shortly before his son was to enroll in university. The family, not rich to begin with, was left impoverished. Once again, Holmboe helped. He contributed money and helped raise additional funds to pay for Abel's education at the University of Christiania. Still under the tutelage of Holmboe, Abel began to do research in advanced mathematics. During his last year at the university, Abel searched for an algorithm that would enable him to solve all algebraic equations of fifth degree. (Recall that an algebraic equation is any equation of the form $a_n x^n + a_{n-1} x^{n-1} + \ldots + a_1 x + a_0 = 0$, where the a_j are rational numbers, called coefficients, and the x^j is the variable x raised to the jth power. The degree of the equation is defined as the highest exponent appearing in the equation. A second-degree, or quadratic, equation, for example, is any equation of the form $a_2 x^2 + a_1 x + a_0 = 0$.) Abel thought that he had found a general solution for all such equations, but he was quickly corrected. Far from being discouraged, he continued to study algebraic equations of degree greater than 4.

After graduation Abel wanted to meet and trade ideas with the best mathematicians in Europe, but there were two problems to overcome. First, he did not speak their languages; second, he had no money. With the help of a small grant he undertook the study of French and German so that he could become fluent enough to engage these mathematicians in conversation. During this time he also proved that there was no general algebraic formula for solving equations of the fifth degree.

Recall that centuries earlier Niccolò Fontana, also known as Tartaglia, had found an algorithm that enabled him to express solutions of any third-degree algebraic equation as a function of the coefficients appearing in the equations. Shortly thereafter Lodovico Ferrari had discovered an algorithm that enabled him to express solutions of any fourth-degree equation as functions of the coefficients. Similar methods for identifying the solutions to all second-degree equations had been discovered even earlier.

Niels Henrik Abel discovered that the search for an algorithm to solve an arbitrary fifth-degree equation was futile; no such algorithm exists. (Library of Congress, Prints and Photographs Division)

What had never been discovered—despite much hard work by many mathematicians—were similar methods that could enable one to express the roots of arbitrary equations of degree higher than 4 as functions of the coefficients. Abel showed that, at least in the case of fifth-degree equations, the long-sought-after formula did not exist. This, he believed, was a demonstration of his talent that would surely attract the attention of the mathematicians he wanted to meet. In 1824 he had the result published in pamphlet form at his own expense, and in 1825 he left Norway with a small sum given him by the Norwegian government to help him in his studies.

He was wrong about the pamphlet. He sent his pamphlet to Carl Friedrich Gauss, but Gauss showed no interest. This is puzzling since Abel had just solved one of the most intractable problems in mathematics. Although Gauss was no help, during the winter of 1825–26, while in Berlin, Abel made the acquaintance of the German mathematician August Leopold Crelle, the publisher of a mathematics journal. Abel and Crelle became friends, and subsequently Crelle published a number of Abel's papers on mathematics, including his work on the insolubility of fifth-degree equations. Abel also traveled to Paris and submitted a paper to the Academy of Sciences. He hoped that this would gain him the recognition that he believed he deserved, but again nothing happened. Throughout much of his travel Abel had found it necessary to borrow money to survive. He eventually found himself deeply in debt, and then he was diagnosed with tuberculosis.

Abel returned to Norway in 1827. Still heavily in debt and without a steady source of income, he began to work as a tutor. Meanwhile news of his discoveries in algebra and other areas of mathematics had spread throughout the major centers of mathematics in Germany and France. Several mathematicians, including Crelle, sought a teaching position for him in the hope of providing Abel with a better environment to study and a more comfortable lifestyle. Meanwhile Abel continued to study mathematics in the relative isolation of his home in Norway. He died before he was offered the job that he so much wanted.

Abel's discovery that not all algebraic equations of degree 5 are solvable is quite technical. It is easier to get a feeling for the new algebra that was developed at this time if we first familiarize ourselves with the research of the main character in this part of the history of algebra, the French mathematician Évariste Galois (1811–32).

Évariste Galois

Today Galois is described as a central figure in the history of mathematics, but during his life he had little contact with other mathematicians. This, however, was not for lack of trying. Galois very much wanted to be noticed.

Évariste Galois was born into a well-to-do family. Nicolas-Gabriel Galois, his father, was active in politics; Adelaide-Marie Demante, his mother, taught Galois at home until he was 12 years old. Because Évariste Galois was dead before his 21st birthday—and because the last several years of his life were extremely turbulent—it is safe to say that he received much of his formal education from his mother. In 1823 Galois enrolled in the Collège Royal de Louis-le-Grand. Initially he gave no evidence of a particular talent for mathematics. Soon, however, he began to do advanced work in mathematics with little apparent preparation. By the time he was 16 he had begun to examine the problem of finding roots to algebraic equations. This problem had already been solved by Abel, but Galois was not aware of this at the time.

Galois was off to a good start, but his luck soon took a turn for the worse. He submitted two formal papers describing his discoveries to the Academy of Sciences in Paris. These papers were sent to the French mathematician Augustin-Louis Cauchy (1789–1857) for review. Cauchy was one of the most prominent mathematicians of his era. He certainly had the imagination and the mathematical skill required to understand Galois's ideas, and a positive review or recommendation from Cauchy would have meant a lot to Galois. Cauchy lost both papers. This occurred in 1829, the same year that Galois's father committed suicide. Eight months later, in 1830, Galois tried again. He submitted another paper on the solution of algebraic equations to the Academy of Sciences. This time the paper was forwarded to the secretary of the academy, the French mathematician and Egyptologist Joseph Fourier (1768–1830). Fourier died before any action was taken on Galois's paper. The paper that was in Fourier's possession was lost as well. Meanwhile Galois had twice applied for admission to the École Polytechnique, which had the best department of mathematics in France. It was certainly the school to attend if one wanted to work as a mathematician. Both times Galois failed to gain admission.

Galois shifted his emphasis and enrolled in the École Normale Supérieure. He hoped to become a teacher of mathematics, but as his father and many of his fellow citizens had, Galois became involved in politics. Politics was important to Galois, and he was not shy about making his ideas known. At the time this activity involved considerable personal risk.

France had been embroiled in political instability and violence since before Galois was even born: The French Revolution began in 1789. It was followed by a period of political terror, during which thousands of people were executed. The military leader and later emperor Napoléon Bonaparte eventually seized power and led French forces on several ultimately unsuccessful campaigns of conquest. The results were the defeat of the French military and Napoléon's imprisonment in 1815. Napoléon's adventurism did nothing to resolve the conflict between those who favored monarchy and those who favored democracy. Galois was one of the latter. In 1830 the reigning French monarch, Charles X, was exiled, but he was replaced with still another monarch. The republicans— Galois among them—were disappointed and angry. Galois wrote an article expressing his ideas and was expelled from the École Normale Supérieure. He continued his activism. He was arrested twice for his views. The second arrest resulted in a six-month jail sentence.

Despite these difficulties Galois did not stop learning about mathematics. In 1831 he tried again. He rewrote his paper and resubmitted it to the academy. This time the paper fell into the hands of the French mathematician Siméon-Denis Poisson (1781–1840). In the history of mathematics, Poisson, like Cauchy and Fourier, is an important figure, but with respect to his handling of Galois's paper, the best that can be said is that he did not lose it. Poisson's review of Galois's paper was brief and to the point: He (Poisson) did not understand it. Because he did not understand it, he could not recommend it for publication. He suggested that the paper be expanded and clarified.

This was the last opportunity Galois had to see his ideas in print. In 1832 at the age of 20 years and seven months, Galois was challenged to a duel. The circumstances of the duel are not entirely clear. Romance and politics are two common, and presumably mutually exclusive, explanations. In any case Galois, although he was sure he would not survive the duel, accepted the challenge. He wrote down his ideas about algebra in a letter to a friend. The contents of the letter were published four months after Galois died in the duel. This was the first publication in the branch of mathematics today known as Galois theory.

Galois Theory and the Doubling of the Cube

To convey some idea of how Galois theory led to a resolution of the three classical unsolved problems in Greek geometry we examine the problem of doubling the cube. Originally the problem was stated as follows: Given a cube, find the dimensions of a second cube whose volume is precisely twice as large as the volume of the first. If we suppose that the length of an edge on the first cube is one unit long, then the volume of the first cube is one cubic unit: Volume = length × width × height. The unit might be a meter, an inch, or a mile; these details have no effect on the problem. If the volume of the original cube is one cubic unit then the problem reduces to finding the dimensions of a cube whose volume is two cubic units. If we suppose that the letter x represents the length of one edge of the larger cube, then the volume of this new cube is x^3, where x satisfies the equation $x^3 = 2$. In other words, $x = \sqrt[3]{2}$, where the notation $\sqrt[3]{2}$ (called the cube root of 2) represents the number that, when cubed, equals 2. The reason that the problem was so difficult is that it called for the construction of a segment of length $\sqrt[3]{2}$ unit *using nothing but a straightedge and compass*. It turns out that this is impossible.

To show that it is not possible to construct a segment of length $\sqrt[3]{2}$ we need two ideas. The first idea is the geometric notion of a constructible number. The second is the

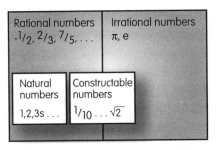

The natural numbers are a subset of the rational numbers. The set of irrational numbers shares no elements with the set of rational numbers. Some constructible numbers are rational and others are irrational. Together the rational numbers and the irrational numbers compose the set of real numbers.

algebraic notion of a field. We begin with an explanation of a constructible number.

We say that a number x is constructible if given a line segment one unit long, we can construct a line segment x units long using only a straightedge and compass. (From now on when we use the word *construct*, we mean "construct using only a straightedge and compass.") A straightedge and compass are very simple implements. There is not much that can be done with them. We can, for example, use the compass to measure the distance between two points by placing the point of the compass on one geometric point and adjusting the compass so that the other point of the compass is on the second geometric point. This creates a "record" of the distance between the points. Also if we are given a line, we can use the compass to construct a second line perpendicular to the first. Besides these there are a few other basic techniques with which every geometry student is familiar. All other geometric constructions are some combination of this handful of basic techniques.

Some numbers are easy to construct. For example, given a segment one unit long, it is easy to construct a segment two units long. One way to accomplish this is to extend the unit line segment, and then use the compass to measure off a second line segment that is one unit long and placed so that it is end to end with the original unit segment. This construction proves that the number 2 is constructible. In a similar way, we can construct a segment that is n units long where n is any natural number. Our first conclusion is that all natural numbers are constructible.

We can also use our straightedge and compass to represent the addition, subtraction, multiplication, and division of natural numbers. To add two natural numbers—which we call m and n—we just construct the two corresponding line segments—one of length m and one of length n—and place them end to end. The result is a line segment of length $m + n$. In a similar way we can represent the difference of the numbers $n - m$: To accomplish this we just measure "out" n units, and "back" m units. It is also true, although we do not show it, that given any two whole numbers m and n, we can construct a line segment of length *mn* and a line segment of length *m/n*, provided, of course, that *n* is not 0. What this indicates is that every rational number is constructible.

Some irrational numbers are also constructible. We can, for example, use a straightedge and compass to construct a square each of whose sides is one unit long. The diagonal of the square is of length $\sqrt{2}$ units long, as an application of the Pythagorean theorem demonstrates. This shows that $\sqrt{2}$ is also a constructible number. We can even construct more complicated-looking numbers. For example, because $\sqrt{2}$ is constructible, we can also construct a line segment of length $1 + \sqrt{2}$. We can use this segment to construct a square with sides of length $1 + \sqrt{2}$. The diagonal of this square is of length $\sqrt{3 + 2\sqrt{2}}$, as another application of the Pythagorean theorem shows. This proves that this more complicated-looking number is constructible as well. These processes can be repeated as many times as desired. The result can be some very complicated-looking numbers. The question then is, Can $\sqrt[3]{2}$ be constructed by some similar sequence of steps?

If we can show that $\sqrt[3]{2}$ is not constructible then we will have demonstrated that it is impossible to double the cube by using a straightedge and compass as our only tools. To do this we need the algebraic concept of a field.

We define a *field* as any set of numbers that is closed under addition, subtraction, multiplication, and division. By *closed* we mean that if we combine any two numbers in the set through the use of one of the four arithmetic operations, the result is another number in the set. For example, the rational numbers form a field, because no matter how we add, subtract, multiply, or divide any pair of rational numbers, the result is always another rational number (provided that we do not divide by 0). Similarly, the real numbers form a field. It turns out, however, that there are many fields that contain all the rational numbers but that do not contain all of the real numbers. Although they are not as familiar as the fields of rational and real numbers, these intermediary fields are the ones that are important to proving the impossibility of doubling the cube.

DOUBLING THE CUBE WITH A STRAIGHTEDGE AND COMPASS IS IMPOSSIBLE

Using the information in the text, we can show how the "new algebra" can be used to complete the proof that it is impossible to construct $\sqrt[3]{2}$ with a straightedge and compass. To appreciate the proof one needs to keep in mind two facts:

1. The number $\sqrt[3]{2}$ is irrational.

2. The graph of the polynomial $y = x^3 - 2$ crosses the x-axis only once.

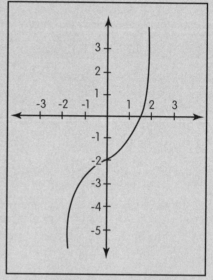

The graph of the curve $y = x^3 - 2$. *Notice that the graph crosses the* x-*axis only once.*

Here is the proof: Suppose that we adjoin $\sqrt{k_1}, \sqrt{k_2}, \sqrt{k_3}, \ldots, \sqrt{k_n}$ to the field of rational numbers, one after another, in the same way that $\sqrt{2}$ and then $\sqrt{a+b\sqrt{2}}$ are adjoined to the rational numbers in the main body of the text. Our hypothesis is that if we adjoin enough of these numbers to the field of rational numbers, we eventually create a field that contains $\sqrt[3]{2}$. (We can use this hypothesis to create two contradictions that prove that doubling the cube with a straightedge and compass is impossible.)

We begin our work with the rational numbers, which we represent with the letter F_0. By fact 1, $\sqrt[3]{2}$ does not belong to F_0 so we have to adjoin at least one number to F_0 in order that our new field will contain $\sqrt[3]{2}$. We adjoin $\sqrt{k_1}$ to the rational numbers (where k_1 belongs to F_0 but $\sqrt{k_1}$ does not) to get a new field that we call F_1. (Every number in F_1 is of the form $a + b\sqrt{k_1}$, where a, b, and k_1 are chosen from F_0, the field of rational numbers.) Next we choose k_2 from F_1 and then adjoin $\sqrt{k_2}$ to F_1 to create a new field, which we call F_2. (The numbers in F_2 are of the form $c + d\sqrt{k_2}$, where c and d represent numbers taken from F_1.) We continue the process until we reach F_n, which is obtained by adjoining

$\sqrt{k_n}$ to the field F_{n-1}. The elements in F_n are of the form $p + q\sqrt{k_n}$, where p, q, and k_n belong to the field F_{n-1}. (The fields are like traditional Russian matryoshka dolls, each one fitting inside a slightly larger one, beginning with the smallest, the field of rational numbers, and ending with the largest, F_n.) We assume that each time we adjoin some $\sqrt{k_j}$ it makes the field to which we adjoin it bigger. In other words, we suppose that it is never the case that $\sqrt{k_j}$ belongs to F_{j-1}, the field from which k_j was drawn. Otherwise every number of the form $e + f\sqrt{k_j}$ would be in F_{j-1} and we would not have made F_{j-1} bigger by adjoining $\sqrt{k_j}$ to it. Finally we assume that we stop as soon as we have a field that contains $\sqrt[3]{2}$. This means that F_n contains $\sqrt[3]{2}$ but F_{n-1} does not.

To prove that the cube cannot be doubled by using a straightedge and compass, we work with the equation $\sqrt[3]{2} = p + q\sqrt{k_n}$. This equation must be true for some numbers p, q, and k_n in the field F_{n-1} because we have assumed that $\sqrt[3]{2}$ lies in F_n and every number in F_n can be written in this form. We use this equation for $\sqrt[3]{2}$ to obtain two contradictions. The contradictions show that the hypothesis that $\sqrt[3]{2}$ belongs to F_n is impossible. Therefore, we have to conclude that the field F_n does not contain $\sqrt[3]{2}$. Since every constructible number belongs to some field of the type F_n, this will prove that $\sqrt[3]{2}$ is not constructible and so the cube cannot be doubled with a straightedge and compass. The computations go like this: Cube both sides of the equation $\sqrt[3]{2} = p + q\sqrt{k_n}$—that is, multiply each side by itself three times—to get $2 = (p^3 + 3q^2k_n) + (3p^2q + b^3k_n)\sqrt{k_n}$. Now consider $(3p^2q + b^3k_n)$, the coefficient of $\sqrt{k_n}$. Contradiction 1: If $(3p^2q + b^3k_n)$ is not equal to 0, then we can solve for $\sqrt{k_n}$ in terms of numbers that all belong to the field F_{n-1}. Since F_{n-1} is a field we conclude that $\sqrt{k_n}$ belongs to F_{n-1} and our assumption that F_n is bigger than F_{n-1} was in error. This is the first contradiction. Contradiction 2: If the number $(3p^2q + b^3k)$ equals 0, then cube the new number $p - q\sqrt{k_n}$ to get $(p^3 + 3q^2k) - (3p^2q + b^3k)\sqrt{k_n}$. Since $(3p^2q + b^3k)$ is 0 it must be the case that $p - q\sqrt{k_n}$ is also a cube root of 2. [Because if $(3p^2q + b^3k)$ is 0 then both the cube of $p - q\sqrt{k_n}$ and the cube of $p + q\sqrt{k_n}$ are equal, and we have already assumed that $p + q\sqrt{k_n}$ is the cube root of 2.] Therefore, the graph of $y = x^3 - 2$ must cross the x axis at $p - q\sqrt{k_n}$ and at $p + q\sqrt{k_n}$. This contradicts fact number 2.

The situation is hopeless. If we assume that $(3p^2q + b^3k)$ is not 0 we get a contradiction. If we assume that $(3p^2q + b^3k)$ is 0 we get a contradiction. This shows that our assumption that we could construct $\sqrt[3]{2}$ was in error, and we have to conclude that $\sqrt[3]{2}$ is not constructible with a straightedge and compass. This is one of the more famous proofs in the history of mathematics.

To see an example of one of these intermediary fields, consider the set of all numbers of the form $a + b\sqrt{2}$, where a and b are chosen from the set of rational numbers. No matter how we add, subtract, multiply, or divide two numbers of the form $a + b\sqrt{2}$ the result is always another number of the same form. This field is called an extension of the rational numbers. We say that we have adjoined $\sqrt{2}$ to the rational numbers to obtain this extension. Every number in the field consisting of $\sqrt{2}$ adjoined to the rational numbers, which we represent with the symbol $Q(\sqrt{2})$, is constructible. (Notice that when $b = 0$ the resulting number is rational. This shows that the field of rational numbers is a subfield of $Q(\sqrt{2})$.)

Having created the extension $Q(\sqrt{2})$ we can use it to make an even larger field by adjoining the square root of some element of $Q(\sqrt{2})$. The element we adjoin is of the form $\sqrt{a + b\sqrt{2}}$. Every number in this field has the form $c + d\sqrt{a + b\sqrt{2}}$, where c and d are chosen from $Q(\sqrt{2})$ and $a + b\sqrt{2}$ is positive. We can do this as often as we want. Each new field can be chosen so that it is larger than the previous one. Every number in each such extension is constructible, and conversely, every constructible number belongs to a field that is formed in this way.

To complete the proof we need only show that no matter how many times we extend the rational numbers in the manner just described, the resulting field never contains the number $\sqrt[3]{2}$. The proof uses the concept of field and requires us to complete a few complicated-looking multiplication problems and recall a bit of analytic geometry (see the sidebar for details).

The Solution of Algebraic Equations

Some fields are smaller than others. To repeat an example already given, the field of rational numbers is "smaller" than the field defined as $Q(\sqrt{2})$, because every number in $Q(\sqrt{2})$ is of the form $a + b\sqrt{2}$ where a and b are rational numbers; if we consider the case where b is 0 and a is any rational number, then it is apparent that $Q(\sqrt{2})$ contains every rational number. However, when $b = 1$ and $a = 0$, we can see that $Q(\sqrt{2})$ also contains $\sqrt{2}$, which is not rational. Because the rational numbers are a proper subset of $Q(\sqrt{2})$, we can say that the field of rational numbers is smaller than $Q(\sqrt{2})$.

For each algebraic equation there is always a smallest field that contains all the roots of the equation. This is the field we obtain by adjoining the smallest possible set of numbers to the set of rational numbers. This field, which is determined by the roots of the polynomial of interest, is important enough to have its own name. It is called the splitting field. Depending on the polynomial, the splitting field can have a fairly complicated structure. The numbers that make up the field can sometimes be difficult to write down; they are usually not constructible; and as do all the fields that we consider, the splitting field contains infinitely many numbers. Furthermore, it must be closed under four arithmetic operations: addition, subtraction, multiplication, and division. Fields are complicated objects. It was one of Galois's great insights that he was able to rephrase the problem of solving algebraic equations so that it was simple enough to solve. His solution involved another type of algebraic structure called a group.

The idea of a group is one of the most important ideas in mathematics. There are many kinds of groups. Galois concentrated on one kind of group, called a permutation group. We can create an example of a permutation group by cutting a square out of the center of a piece of paper. Suppose that, by moving clockwise about the square, we number each of the corners as shown. Suppose, too, that we number the corresponding corners of the square hole from which the square was cut so that when we replace the square inside the square hole, each number on the square matches up with its mate (see Figure [A]).

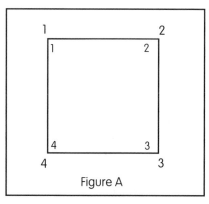

Figure A

Figure A, the identity permutation.

If we now rotate the square 90° clockwise about its center, the number 1 on the square matches up with the number 2 on the hole. The number 2 on the square matches the number 3 on the hole, and so on (see Figure [B]).

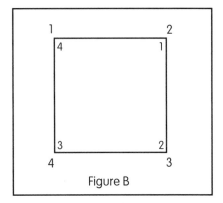

Figure B

Figure B, a 90° clockwise rotation.

If we rotate that square 180° out of its original position, we get a new configuration (see Figure [C]).

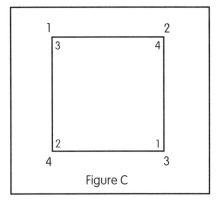

Figure C

Figure C, a 180° clockwise rotation.

There are two other rotations that are possible. One entails rotating the square 270° clockwise—this yields a fourth configuration (see Figure [D])—and the last rotation entails rotating the square 360° clockwise (see Figure [A] again). Notice that making the last rotation has the same effect as not moving the square at all.

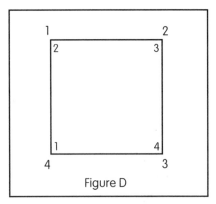

Figure D

Figure D, a 270° clockwise rotation.

All four of these rotations taken together form a *group:* No matter whether we rotate the square once and then follow that rotation by another rotation—no matter whether we rotate the square many times—the result always reduces to one of the rotations we have already described. We have created a physical representation of a group with four elements.

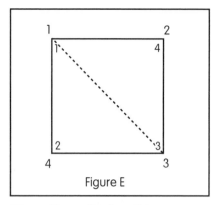

Figure E

Figure E, a reflection of the square about the line connecting corners 1 and 3.

The four-element group described in the previous paragraph is also a *subgroup*—that is, it is a group that is part of a larger group of motions of the square. We can get more motions in our group by "reflecting" the square about a line of symmetry. Physically this can be accomplished by flipping the square over along one of its lines of symmetry. For example, we can flip the square along the line connecting two opposite corners. Under these circumstances two corners of the square remain motionless while the other two corners swap places. If, for example, we reflect the square about the line connecting the corners 1 and 3, then corners 2 and 4 of the square change places while 1 and 3 remain motionless (see Figure [E]). This configuration (corners 1 and 3 fixed and corners 2 and 4 exchanged) is new; we cannot obtain this reflection through any sequence of rotations, but it is far from the only reflection that we can

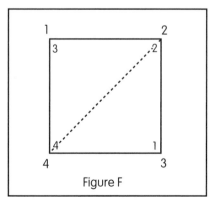

Figure F

Figure F, a reflection of the square about the line connecting corners 2 and 4.

generate. We can obtain still another configuration of the square within its hole by reflecting the square about its other diagonal (see Figure [F]). There are two other reflections—each is obtained by reflecting the square about lines passing through the center of the square and the midpoint of a side. We omit the details. Allowing all possible combinations of rotations and reflections gives us a still larger group. (Of course, there are mathematical formulas that do the same thing that we are doing with paper, but the mathematical methods are simply a symbolic substitute for rotating the square through multiples of 90° and reflecting it about its axes of symmetry.)

So far we have examined only the motions obtainable by rotating and reflecting a square, but we can generate other, very different, permutation groups by using other geometric figures. Depending on the figures we choose to study, the permutation groups we generate may have more or fewer elements than the permutation group associated with the square. The subgroups associated with each permutation group also depend on the group that we study. Galois did not invent permutation groups, but he did find an extraordinarily creative use for them.

Galois noticed that to each (infinite) splitting field there corresponds a unique (finite) permutation group. The algebraic structure of two splitting fields is "the same" if they have the same permutation group. Even better, the permutation group contains important information about the splitting field and the algebraic equation from which the field is obtained. In particular, an algebraic equation can be solved if the permutation group has a certain structure. If the permutation group lacks this structure then there is no algorithm analogous to those discovered by Tartaglia and Ferrari that would enable one to solve the equation.

It might seem as if Galois simply swapped the difficulties of working with algebraic equations for the difficulties of working with splitting fields, then swapped the problems he encountered with splitting fields for a new set of problems associated with groups. There is, however, a real advantage to studying the permutation group instead of the splitting field or the algebraic equation: The group problem is simple enough to solve. Unlike the

GROUP THEORY IN CHEMISTRY

A. Identity

B. Reflection about dotted line

C. $180°$ rotation

Three elements in the symmetry group of the molecule ethene.

Symmetries are everywhere. Humans are (approximately) bilaterally symmetric in the sense that the left side of the human body is a mirror image of the right side. This is why a good portrait artist can accurately "complete" a portrait, given, for example, only the left half of a picture of the subject's face, but cannot do as well when provided with a picture of, for example, the lower half of the face. Large trees with many branches are often rotationally symmetric in the sense that if they could be rotated about a vertical line passing through the center of the trunk, they would look essentially the same after the rotation as before. A five-petal flower, for example, is somewhat more symmetric than a person and less symmetric than a large tree: If a flower is rotated clockwise or counterclockwise about its vertical axis by any multiple of $72°$, the flower looks "the same" in the

(continues)

GROUP THEORY IN CHEMISTRY
(continued)

sense that we cannot detect whether or not a rotation took place. The restriction to 72° (72° = 360°/5) is necessary, because a rotation by a multiple of 72° moves each petal into the position occupied by some other petal.

A transformation that leaves an object looking the same after the transformation as it did before is a *symmetry transformation*. Chemists are often concerned with transformations that leave a molecule looking the same after a transformation as it looked before. This type of analysis is an important application of group theory. The first step in using group theory in the study of molecules is to identify all of the symmetry transformations associated with a molecule.

Figure A shows the structure of the molecule ethene. Each line represents an electron shared by two atoms. The letters C and H stand for carbon and hydrogen atoms, respectively. The diagram indicates that ethene consists of two carbon and four hydrogen atoms. The numbers attached to each letter are just a convenience: They are used so that we can distinguish between atoms that are of the same type and therefore otherwise indistinguishable. Figure A also shows the simplest of all symmetry transformations: If we do nothing then the molecule looks the same before we did nothing as it did afterward. This not-very-interesting transformation is called the identity transformation. Figure B shows that if we reflect the diagram about the dotted line, the atom H_1 exchanges places with H_2, atom H_3 exchanges places with H_4, and the two carbon atoms exchange places as well. If we had not attached numbers to the letters we could not know that the reflection had occurred at all. This reflection, therefore, belongs to the set of symmetry transformations associated with ethene. Figure C shows that if the entire molecule is rotated clockwise about its center the two carbon molecules exchange places, H_1 exchanges places with H_3, and H_2 exchanges places with H_4, so this rotation is also a symmetry transformation. Other symmetry transformations are associated with ethene as well.

To every molecule we can associate a symmetry group. When two different molecules have the same basic shape, they also have the same symmetry group. Consequently it is possible to categorize molecules on the basis of their symmetry group—two molecules with the same symmetry group belong to the same class. Symmetry groups and their associated calculations enable chemists to predict many important molecular properties, interpret data, and simplify complex theories. Symmetry groups have proved to be an important concept in theoretical chemistry.

splitting fields, which have four operations and infinitely many numbers, each permutation group has only one operation and finitely many elements. Galois swapped a harder problem for an easier problem. The group problem was manageable; the field problem was not.

This is an example of what is meant by *structure* in mathematics. Each splitting field has many properties in common with other fields—that is why they are all called fields—but there are differences between the fields as well. These finer points of structure are determined by the nature of the roots that are adjoined to the rational numbers in order to get the splitting field. The finer points of structure in the field determine the properties of the permutation group. In this sense the structure of the group reflects the structure of the field, but, because the group is easier to understand, solving problems associated with the field by studying its associated permutation group becomes possible.

The discovery of these group methods required an especially creative mathematical mind. Galois's ideas represented a huge leap forward in mathematical thinking, and it would be some time before other mathematicians caught up. Today groups are one of the central concepts in all of mathematics. They play a prominent role in geometry, analysis, algebra, probability, and many branches of applied science as well. The search for the structures that underlie mathematics, and the search for criteria—analogous to Galois's permutation groups—that enable mathematicians to determine when two structures are really "the same" are now central themes of algebraic research. In many ways these ideas are responsible for the ever-increasing pace of mathematical progress. What we now call modern, or abstract, algebra begins with the work of a French teenager almost 200 years ago.

7

THE LAWS OF THOUGHT

Algebra changed radically more than once during the 19th century. Previously Descartes had interpreted his variables as magnitudes, that is, lengths of line segments. He used algebra as a tool in his study of geometry. Leibniz and Newton had interpreted the variables that arose in their computations as geometric magnitudes or as forces or accelerations. On the one hand, these interpretations helped them state their mathematical questions in a familiar context. They enabled Newton and Leibniz to discover new relationships among the symbols in their equations, so in this sense these interpretations were useful. On the other hand, these interpretations were not necessary. One can study the equations of interest to Descartes, Newton, and Leibniz without imposing any extramathematical interpretation on the symbols employed. At the time no one thought to do this.

In the 19th century mathematicians began to look increasingly inward. They began to inquire about the true subject matter of mathematics. The answer for many of them was that mathematics was solely concerned with the relationships among symbols. They were not interested in what the symbols represented, only in the rules that governed the ways symbols were combined. To many people, even today, this sounds sterile. What is surprising is that their inquiries about the relationships among symbols resulted in some very important, practical applications, the most notable of which is the digital computer.

Aristotle

The new and more abstract concept of mathematics began in the branch of knowledge called logic. Logic began with the works of the ancient Greek philosopher Aristotle (384 B.C.E.–322 B.C.E.). Aristotle was educated at the academy of the philosopher Plato, which was situated in Athens. He arrived at the academy at the age of 17 and remained until Plato's death 20 years later. When Plato died, Aristotle left Athens and traveled for the next 12 years. He taught in different places and established two schools. Finally he returned to Athens, and at the age of 50 he established the school for which he is best remembered, the Lyceum. Aristotle taught there for the next 12 years. The Lyceum was

Aristotle. His ideas about logic were central to Western thinking for 2,000 years. (Topham/The Image Works)

a place that encouraged free inquiry and research. Aristotle himself taught numerous subjects and wrote about what he discovered. For Aristotle all of this abruptly ended in 323 B.C.E., when Alexander the Great died. There was widespread resentment of Alexander in Athens, and Aristotle, who had been Alexander's tutor, felt the wrath of the public directed at him after the death of his former student. Aristotle left Athens under threat of violence. He died one year later.

One of the subjects in which Aristotle was interested was logic, that branch of thought that deals with the "laws" of correct reasoning. Aristotle's contribution to logic was his study of something called the syllogism. This is a very formal, carefully defined type of reasoning. It begins with categorical statements, usually called categorical propositions. A proposition is a simple statement. "The car is black" is an example of a proposition. Many other types of sentences are not categorical propositions. "Do you wish you had a black car?" and "Buy the black car" are examples of statements that are not propositions. These types of sentences are not part of Aristotle's inquiry. Instead his syllogisms are defined only for the categorical proposition.

A categorical proposition is a statement of relationship between two classes. "All dogs are mammals" is an example of a categorical proposition. It states that every creature in the class of dogs also belongs to the class of mammals. We can form other categorical propositions about the class of dogs and the class of mammals. Some are more sensible than others:

- "Some dogs are mammals."
- "No dogs are mammals."
- "Some dogs are not mammals."

are all examples of categorical propositions. We can strip away the content of these four categorical propositions about the class of dogs and the class of mammals and consider the four general *types* of categorical expressions in a more abstract way:

- All x's are y's.
- Some x's are y's.
- No x's are y's.
- Some x's are not y's.

Here we can either let the xs represent dogs and the ys represent mammals or let the letters represent some other classes. We can even refrain from assigning any extramathematical meaning at all to the letters.

We can use the four types of categorical propositions to form one or more syllogisms. A syllogism consists of three categorical propositions. The first two propositions are premises. The third proposition is the conclusion. Here is an example of a syllogism:

- Premise 1: All dogs are mammals.
- Premise 2: All poodles are dogs.
- Conclusion: All poodles are mammals.

We can form similar sorts of syllogisms by using the other three types of categorical propositions. In all, we can form 256 different types of syllogisms from the four types of categorical propositions, but only 24 of the syllogisms are logically valid.

Aristotle's writings were collected and edited by Andronicus of Rhodes, the last head of Aristotle's Lyceum. This occurred about three centuries after Aristotle's death. The *Organon*, as Andronicus named it, is the collection of Aristotle's writings on logic. It became one of the most influential books in the history of Western thought.

Aristotle's ideas on logic were studied, copied, and codified by medieval scholars. They formed an important part of the educational curriculum in Renaissance Europe. In fact, the *Organon* formed a core part of many students' education into the 20th century. But the syllogism tells us little about the current state of logic. Its importance is primarily historical: For about 2,000 years the syllogism was the principal object of study for those interested in logic. For 20 centuries not one new idea on logic was added to those of Aristotle. Many scholars thought that, at least in the area of logic, Aristotle had done all that could be done. They believed that in the area of logic no new discoveries were possible.

There is no doubt that Aristotle made an important contribution to understanding logic, because his was the first contribution. In retrospect, however, Aristotle's insights were very limited. Logic is more than the syllogism, because language is more than a set of syllogisms. Logic and language are closely related. We can express ourselves logically in a variety of ways, and not every set of logical statements can be reduced to a collection of syllogisms. Aristotle had found a way of expressing certain logical arguments, but his insights are just too simple to be generally useful.

Gottfried Leibniz

The German philosopher, mathematician, and diplomat Gottfried Wilhelm Leibniz was born in 1646 in Leipzig, a region of Europe devastated by the Thirty Years' War (1618–48). When Leibniz was just a boy, his father died. The elder Leibniz left behind a personal library where his son spent many long hours as he was growing up. Though Leibniz attended school it is believed that he acquired most of his early education from his father's books.

Leibniz learned of the work of Descartes and Galileo at the University of Leipzig, where he studied law. He was denied a doctorate from Leipzig, apparently because, at the age of 20, he was thought too young. Leibniz left Leipzig and submitted a thesis to the University of Altdorf. It was quickly accepted. Altdorf awarded him a doctorate and offered him a position on the faculty, but Leibniz refused the position. He became a diplomat instead.

When Leibniz was a young man, Europe was rebuilding. Evidence of the Thirty Years' War, which had had its roots partly in religious strife, was everywhere. The Continent was on the mend. New ideas about mathematics and science were spreading across the land. Leibniz, who had an extraordinarily broad intellect, strove to learn as much as he could. Nor was his attention fixed solely on math and science. He was also interested in philosophy, law, history, and languages. There was, in fact, little that escaped his attention. He is often described as the last person who truly mastered all academic disciplines of his age.

Leibniz's broad interests were reflected in his very broad and ambitious goals. When faced with diversity, Leibniz sought unity. This seems to have been part of his personality. It is sometimes speculated that the reason he rejected a position on the faculty at Altdorf is that he could not tolerate the segmentation of knowledge that is characteristic of much of academic work. During his university days Leibniz sought to unify and reconcile the classical ideas of Aristotle with the new sciences of his time. Throughout his adult life he attempted to reunite various branches of the Christian religion, and he wanted to unify science. His efforts in this regard are what make him an important figure in the history of logic and the mathematical laws of thought.

Progress in mathematics and science was hindered, according to Leibniz, because the research community was itself fragmented in very fundamental ways. Then, as now, Europe was linguistically fragmented. The spread of scientific discoveries was certainly hampered by linguistic barriers. Further, scientists sometimes disagreed about the validity of a particular theory not because they differed about the quality of the available evidence, but because they could not agree on what constituted acceptable proof. Leibniz proposed the establishment of a specialized language of science. His method was twofold. First, he sought to develop a set of universal symbols that would enable scientists to communicate across linguistic barriers. This would speed and clarify communication. Second, he sought to develop a set of rules that would enable every user of this new vocabulary to manipulate the symbols in a transparent and logical way.

Leibniz's proposal for a universal language of science is more than a linguistic preference. His idea also contains certain important philosophical assumptions about the nature of knowledge. Philosophically Leibniz believed in the possibility of isolating a relatively small number of fundamental concepts on which higher knowledge is based. These fundamental concepts were to be the building blocks of his linguistic system.

Each concept would, according to Leibniz, be represented by an *ideogram*, which is just another word for symbol. More complex ideas would then be represented by various combinations of this fundamental set of ideograms. In this way scientists and mathematicians could build knowledge by (correctly) combining symbols in new ways. Leibniz, however, offered little guidance on the means of choosing concepts that are sufficiently fundamental to deserve to be represented by their own ideograms. Nor did he deal with the problem of what to do if two philosophers or scientists choose different sets of fundamental concepts with which to begin their studies.

If we assume that all interested parties can agree on a single set of fundamental concepts with which to begin, then the second aspect of Leibniz's program can be implemented. This involved mathematics. Mathematically Leibniz wanted to devise a specialized set of rules for manipulating the ideograms. He wanted to develop a calculus of reasoning or a "universal calculus." The universal calculus would enable the user to arrive at new deductions in a way that was transparent and, if properly done, correct. In Leibniz's vision the universal calculus would make it possible to reduce research to calculations with ideograms in much the same way that research into certain branches of mathematics has been reduced to the manipulation of symbols according to certain generally accepted rules. This was the first attempt at developing an algebra of thought.

Although we have concentrated on Leibniz's ideas as they applied to mathematics and science, his conception was actually much broader. Leibniz was searching for very general laws of thought as well as the vocabulary needed to express those laws. Essentially Leibniz hoped that disagreements of all sorts could be settled via computations.

Had he been successful, Leibniz would have been able to translate the long prose discourses of the mathematicians of his day into a concise set of symbolic relations. In particular, Aristotle's syllogisms could have been expressed in a few lines consisting of a few symbols each. It was an ambitious plan, and Leibniz worked throughout his life to interest other scientists in adopting his ideas, because no single individual can bring about linguistic change by adopting a language understood only by him or her. The results of his efforts were mixed.

Leibniz's conception of a scientific language combined with a universal calculus was not adopted by his contemporaries. Nor can it be adopted today—not, at least, as Leibniz conceived it. The reason is that Leibniz's vision is, in a sense, excessively mathematical. Mathematical arguments are deductive in nature, and deduction is only one kind of reasoning. Deductive reasoning is drawing specific conclusions from general principles. When mathematicians reason deductively, they discover new results, called theorems, by drawing conclusions from previously proved theorems, from definitions, and from the axioms that describe the mathematical system in which they are interested. (Axioms are the statements that determine the nature of a mathematical system. They are not subject to proof.) Of all branches of human knowledge, only mathematics depends so heavily on deductive reasoning. Leibniz's system of knowledge was a deductive system. By contrast, science depends more on induction, which often involves drawing general conclusions from numerous individual observations. This is not only true now; it was true during Leibniz's time. The primacy of the experimental method (essentially a kind of induction) over deductive reasoning was a principle that Galileo worked hard to establish before Leibniz was even born. Leibniz, however, left little room in his algebra of thought for inductive reasoning.

Despite the fact that Leibniz's grand vision was flawed, fragments of the system that he envisioned can be found in various branches of knowledge. Mathematics, for example, makes use of a number of ideograms to represent certain fundamental concepts, and they are understood by mathematicians around the world and from culture to culture. Similarly the same combinations of letters and numbers used to express the chemical composition of various compounds are well understood across linguistic and cultural groups. These symbols can be combined to represent chemical reactions, but not every combination of symbols represents a reaction. They can be correctly combined only in certain ways. The possibility of certain chemical reactions can be ruled out simply because the symbols "do not compute." Finally, Leibniz was the first person to contribute, in a very general way, to the development of the laws of thought that are used in the design of integrated circuits—the circuits that, for example, make it possible for computers to process data—so in this respect, Leibniz's ideas have important practical applications as well. Good ideas, however, are in themselves seldom sufficient. What was necessary was someone with the mathematical insight and ambition to grapple with the very difficult problems involved in implementing an algebra of thought.

George Boole and the Laws of Thought

The 20th-century British philosopher and mathematician Bertrand Russell wrote that modern, "pure" mathematics began with the work of the British mathematician George Boole (1815–64). Not everyone agrees with Russell's assessment, but there can be little doubt that Boole, a highly original thinker, contributed many insights that have proved to be extremely important in ways both theoretical and practical. Nor can there be any doubt that he was, even by today's standards, a pure mathematician. The following famous quotation, taken from his article "Mathematical Analysis of Logic," strikes many contemporary readers as radical in that he insists that mathematics is about nothing more than the relationships among symbols:

> They who are acquainted with the present state of the theory of Symbolical Algebra, are aware, that the validity of the processes of analysis does not depend upon the interpretation of the symbols which are employed, but solely upon the laws of their combination. Every system of interpretation which does not affect the truth of the relations supposed, is equally admissible, and it is thus that the same process may, under one scheme of interpretation, represent the solution of a question on the properties of numbers, under another, that of a geometrical problem, and under a third, that of a problem of dynamics or optics. This principle is indeed of fundamental importance; and it may with safety be affirmed, that the recent advances of pure analysis have been much assisted by the influence which it has exerted in directing the current of investigation.
>
> (Boole, George. Mathematical Analysis of Logic: being an essay towards a calculus of deductive reasoning. Oxford: B. Blackwell, 1965)

Despite Boole's assertion that mathematics is about nothing more than symbolic relationships, Boole's insights have since found important applications, especially in the area of computer chip design.

Boole was born into a poor family. His father was a cobbler, who was interested in science, mathematics, and languages. His interest in these subjects was purely intellectual. He enjoyed learning, and he put his discoveries to use by designing and then creating various optical instruments; telescopes, microscopes, and cameras were all produced in the elder Boole's workshop. As a youth George Boole helped his father in the workshop, and it was from these experiences presumably that he developed an interest in the science of optics, a subject about which he wrote as an adult.

Despite their poverty, the Booles sent their son to various schools. These schools were not especially distinguished, but he learned a great deal from his father, and he supplemented all of this with a lot of independent study. He read about history and science; he enjoyed biographies, poetry, and fiction; and as many of the mathematicians described in this history did, Boole displayed an unusual facility with language. While a teenager, and despite a good deal of adversity, he learned Latin, Greek, French, Italian,

George Boole, founder of Boolean algebra. (Topham/The Image Works)

and German. His interest in learning languages began early. At the age of 14 he translated a poem from Latin to English and had the result published in a local newspaper. The publication of the translation set off a minor controversy when one reader wrote to the newspaper to question whether anyone so young could have produced such a skillful translation. Boole was clearly an outstanding student, but his formal education was cut short.

In 1831 when Boole was 16, his father's business became bankrupt. The penalties for bankruptcy were more serious then than they are now, and George Boole left school to help his family. He got a job, first as an assistant teacher, and later as a teacher. It was at this time that he began to concentrate his energy on learning mathematics. He later explained that he turned toward mathematics because at the time he could not afford to buy many books, and mathematics books, which required more time to be read, offered better value. Throughout this period of independent study Boole went through several teaching jobs. At the age of 20 when he had saved enough money, he opened his own boarding school in his hometown of Lincoln.

It is a tribute to his intellectual ambition and his love of mathematics that despite moving from job to job and later establishing and operating his own school, Boole found enough time to learn higher mathematics and to publish his ideas. He also began to make contacts with university professors so that he could discuss mathematics with other experts. Eventually Boole was awarded the Royal Society of London's first Gold Medal for one of his mathematics papers.

Boole never did attend college. His formal education ended permanently when he left school at the age of 16. Not everyone has the drive to overcome this kind of educational isolation, but it seemed to suit Boole. Unlike many of his university-trained contemporaries, Boole had considerable language skills that enabled him to read important mathematical works in their original languages. He developed unique insights in both mathematics and philosophy. Soon Boole turned away from the type of mathematics that would have been familiar to every mathematician of Boole's time and directed his energy toward discovering what he called the "laws of thought."

Boole's inquiry into the laws of thought is a mathematical and philosophical analysis of formal logic, often called symbolic logic, logic, or, sometimes, logistic. The field of logic deals with the principles of reasoning. It contains Aristotle's syllogisms as a very special case, but Boole's inquiry extended far beyond anything that Aristotle envisioned. Having developed what was essentially a new branch of mathematics, Boole longed for more time to explore these ideas further. His duties at his own school as well as other duties at other local schools were enough to keep him very busy but not very well off. When Queen's College (now University College) was established in Cork, Ireland, Boole applied for a teaching position at the new institution. Between the time that he applied and the time that he was hired, three years passed. He had despaired of ever being offered the position, but in 1849 when he finally was, he accepted it and made the most of it.

Boole remained at Queen's College for the rest of his life. He married, and by all accounts he was extremely devoted to his wife. He was apparently regarded with both affection and curiosity by his neighbors: When Boole met anyone who piqued his curiosity, he immediately invited that person to his home for supper and conversation. He is often described as someone who was kind, generous, and extremely inquisitive. Boole died after a brief illness at the age of 49.

Boolean Algebra

Boole's great contribution to mathematics is symbolic logic. Boole sought a way of applying algebra to express and greatly extend classical logic. Recall that Aristotle's syllogisms were a way of making explicit certain simple logical relations between classes of objects. Boole's symbolic logic can do the same thing, but his concept of logic greatly extended Aristotle's ideas by using certain logical *operators* to explore and express the relations between various classes. His approach to logic depended on three "simple" operators, which we (for now) denote by AND, OR, and NOR. Over the intervening years, mathematicians have found it convenient to modify some of Boole's own ideas about these operators, but initially we restrict our attention to Boole's definitions. For purposes of this exposition it is sufficient to restrict our attention to careful definitions of the operators AND and OR.

Definition of AND: Given two classes, which we call x and y, the expression xANDy denotes the set of all elements that are common to both the classes x and y. For example, if x represents the class of all cars and y represents the set of all objects that are red, then xANDy represents the class of all red cars. This notation is hardly satisfactory, however, because Boole was interested in developing an *algebra* of thought. As a consequence Boole represented what we have written as xANDy as the "logical product" of x and y, namely, xy. This leads to the first unique aspect of Boole's algebra. Because the set of all elements common to the class x is the class x itself— that is, xANDx *is* x—Boole's algebra has the property that $xx = x$ or, using exponents to express this idea, $x^2 = x$. By repeating this argument multiple times we arrive at the statement $x^n = x$, where n represents any natural number. This equation does not generally hold true in the algebra that we first learn in junior and senior high school, but that does not make it wrong. It is, in fact, one of the defining properties of Boolean algebra. Finally, notice that with this definition of a logical product, the following statement is true: $xy = yx$. That is, the elements that belong to the class xANDy are identical to the elements that belong to the class yANDx.

Definition of OR: Boole's definition of the operator OR is different from that used in Boolean algebra today, but it coincides with one common usage of the word *or*. To appreciate Boole's definition of the operator OR, imagine that we are traveling through the country and arrive at a fork in the road. We have a decision to make: We can turn left or we can turn right. We cannot, however, simultaneously turn both left and right. In this sense, the word *or* is used in a way that is exclusive. We can take one action or the other but not both. Boole defined the OR operator in this exclusive sense. Given two classes, which we call x and y, the expression xORy means the set of elements that are in x but not in y together with the set of elements that are in y but not in x. In particular, the class xORy does not contain any elements that are in x and y. If we again let x represent the class of all cars, and y represent the class of all objects that are red, then the class xORy contains all cars that are not red and every object that is red provided it is not a car. As we have written xORy, Boole used the expression $x + y$. Notice that with this interpretation of the symbol + it is still true that $x + y = y + x$. (We emphasize that Boole's definition of the OR operator is different from the definition in common use today. See the section Refining and Extending Boolean Algebra later in this chapter for a discussion of the difference.)

The axioms for Boole's algebra can now be expressed as follows. A Boolean algebra is, according to Boole, any theory that satisfies the following three equations:

1. $xy = yx$
2. $x(y + z) = xy + xz$
3. $x^n = x$, *where n is any natural number*

The first and third axioms have already been discussed. The meaning of the second axiom can best be explained via a Venn diagram (see the accompanying illustration).

The roles of the numbers 0 and 1 are especially important in Boole's algebra. The number 0 represents the empty set. If, for example, x represents the set of diamonds and y represents the set of emeralds, then xy, the set of objects that are both diamonds and emeralds, is empty—that is, with this interpretation of x and y, $xy = 0$. For Boole, the number 1 represents the *universe* under consideration, that is, the entire class of objects being considered. If we continue to let x represent the set of diamonds and y the set of emeralds, and if, in addition, we let 1 represent the set of all gemstones then we obtain the following three additional equations: (1) $1x = x$, (2) $1y = y$, and (3) $x(1 - y) = x$, where the expression $(1 - y)$ represents all the objects in the universal set that are not emeralds, so that the class of diamonds AND the class of gems that are not emeralds is simply the class of diamonds.

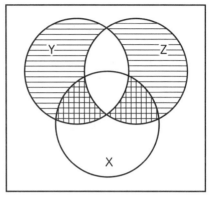

Venn diagram demonstrating that in Boolean algebra $x(y + z) = xy + xz$. Note that $(y + z)$ is the horizontally shaded area, and $x(y + z)$ is the intersection of the horizontally shaded are with x. Alternatively, xy is the area common to disk x and disk y, xz is the area common to disk x and disk z, and $xy + xz$ is the union of xy and xz minus their common area. Therefore, $x(y + z) = xy + xz$.

Recall that in the excerpt from Boole quoted at the beginning of this chapter, he explicitly states, ". . . the validity of the processes of analysis does not depend upon the interpretation of the symbols which are employed." Having established the basic properties of his algebra, he is free to interpret the symbols in any manner convenient. This is important because there was another interpretation that Boole had in mind, and this interpretation has since become very important as well. To appreciate Boole's second interpretation, we imagine some proposition, which we call X, and we let the letter x represent the times when

ARISTOTLE AND BOOLE

For more than 2,000 years Aristotle's treatment of logic was not modified in any significant way. For Western scholars Aristotle's logic was the only type of logic. When propositions are written in ordinary language, understanding why they arrived at this conclusion is not difficult. Written rhetorically, Aristotle's syllogisms have no obvious generalizations. This changed entirely with the work of Boole. Boole's insights enabled him to show that Aristotle's conception was not only limited but also easily extended. Once Aristotle's treatment of the syllogism was expressed by using Boole's algebra, it was seen to be a particularly simple set of computations, and Aristotle's insights were seen to be a very small part of a much larger algebraic landscape.

In the following we list Aristotle's four categorical propositions. Each proposition is followed, in parentheses, by the same expression using Boole's algebra. Following Boole, we use the letter v to represent a nonempty class of objects:

- All x's are y's. ($xy = x$)
- Some x's are y's. ($v = xy$)
- No x's are y's. ($xy = 0$)
- Some x's are not y's. ($v = x(1 - y)$)

Notice that each proposition has been expressed as a simple algebraic equation.

proposition X is true. Because a proposition is either true or false—it cannot be both true and false—the expression $1 - x$ must represent those times when X is false. For example, suppose we let X represent the statement "It is raining." Because we let x represent the times when statement X is true, x represents those times when it actually is raining. The expression $1 - x$ holds when the statement X is false: That is, $1 - x$ represents those times when it is not raining.

In a similar way we can interpret the logical product and the logical sum. If we have two propositions—we represent them with X and Y—then we can let the letter x represent those times when proposition X is true and y represent those times when proposition

Using Boole's algebra, we can express any syllogism via a set of algebraic equations. To illustrate, we rewrite the syllogism given near the beginning of this chapter involving mammals, dogs, and poodles. This requires three equations. Each line of the syllogism is written in words followed, in parentheses, by an algebraic equation that expresses the same idea. We let the letters m, d, and p represent mammals, dogs, and poodles, respectively.

- Premise 1: All dogs are mammals. ($dm = d$)
- Premise 2: All poodles are dogs. ($pd = p$)
- All poodles are mammals. ($pm = p$)

Notice that if we multiply the first equation by p we get $pdm = pd$, but pd equals p by the second equation. All that remains for us to do is write p in place of pd on the left and right in the equation $pdm = pd$. This yields the conclusion of the syllogism, namely, $pm = p$. This example shows how a syllogism can be reduced to an algebraic computation.

This kind of computation is exactly the sort of thing that Leibniz had hoped to accomplish—language as mathematics—but did not bring to fruition. Of course, Boole's goal is a more limited one than that of Leibniz. Unlike Leibniz, who hoped for a universal scientific language, Boole directed his efforts toward expressing logic in the language of algebra. This more focused ambition together with a very creative imagination enabled him to succeed where Leibniz did not.

Y is true. The logical product xy now represents those times when propositions X and Y are *simultaneously* true. For example, let X represent the proposition "It is raining" and let Y represent the statement "It is windy." The expression xy represents those times when it is simultaneously rainy and windy. If we let the number 1 represent a true statement and the number 0 represent a false statement, we obtain the following four equations for the logical product: $1 \times 1 = 1$, $1 \times 0 = 0$, $0 \times 1 = 0$, and $0 \times 0 = 0$. These equations are summarized in a *truth table* where we let T stand for a true statement and F for a false statement, to better reflect the interpretation of Boole's algebra that we have in mind (see the accompanying table). In a similar way, the logical sum $x + y$ represents

AND	T	F
T	T	F
F	F	F

Truth table for the operation AND.

those times when, according to Boole, either proposition X is true or proposition Y is true, but *not* when they are simultaneously true. In our weather example, $x + y$ represents those times when it is either windy or rainy but not both.

Keep in mind that this in no way changes Boole's algebra. According to Boole, mathematics is only about the relationships among symbols, so from a mathematical perspective the interpretation that we place on the symbols is irrelevant. From the point of view of applications, however, the interpretation that we place on the symbols means everything, because it determines how we *use* the algebra. Boole's alternative interpretation of his algebraic symbols as representing true and false values has important applications. It enables one to calculate the true or false values associated with a question or even a chain of equations. Engineers use these ideas to design logic circuits for computers.

Boole's applications of his algebra centered on the theory of probability and the philosophy of mind. Both applications are of a philosophical nature, and they are not well remembered now, principally because Boole's work in these two areas, although intellectually interesting, did not uncover much that was new even at the time. The principal application of Boolean algebra, which involves the design of computer hardware and software, would not be discovered until the 20th century.

Refining and Extending Boolean Algebra

Boole's conception was an important step forward, but it contained some logical problems of its own. The first difficulty was identified and corrected by the British logician and economist

William Stanley Jevons (1835–82). The difficulty arises in the course of computations.

In mathematics—especially pure mathematics—the method by which we arrive at a solution is at least as important as the solution itself. When solving a math problem, any sequence of steps should have the property that *each step can be logically justified.* To express the same idea in a different way: There is a mathematical reason for every step in the solution. This was not the case in Boole's own version of Boolean algebra, and much of the difficulty centered around Boole's definition of the OR operator.

Recall that given two classes of objects, which we call x and y, Boole defined $x + y$ to mean that class of objects that belongs to x or to y but not to both. The problem with this definition is that as one uses Boole's algebra to solve problems, one sometimes encounters expressions such as $x + x$. To obtain this expression, we just substitute the letter x for the letter y in the first sentence of this paragraph. We get that $x + x$ is *that class of objects that belongs to x or to x but not to both.* This is meaningless. Although Boole found ways to manipulate the expressions to obtain valid results, from a logical point of view his definition is not entirely satisfactory. Jevons proposed a new definition for the OR operator, and it is his definition that is in general use today.

Jevons defined the OR operator inclusively: Given two classes, which we call x and y, the expression xORy means the set of objects that are either in x or in y. In particular, Jevons defined OR so that if an object is both in x and in y it also belongs to xORy. The main advantage of Jevons's definition is that it allows us to attach a reasonable definition to the expression $x + x$: The set of objects belonging to the class xORx equals the class x itself. Admittedly this sounds stilted, but it allows us to attach a meaning to the expression $x + x$ that is logically satisfactory. In particular, this definition enables us to write the equation $x + x = x$. This is a different sort of equation than the one we encounter in our first algebra courses, but it parallels Boole's own equation for logical multiplication, namely, $x^2 = x$. This new definition of the OR operator straightened out many of the logical difficulties that had arisen in computing with Boole's algebra.

Notice, too, that in the equations $x + x = x$ and $x^2 = x$ the only coefficient to occur is 1. Furthermore if we search for roots of the equation $x^2 - x = 0$, we find that the only roots are the numbers 0 and 1. In other words, these equations enable us to restrict our attention to just two digits. This turns out to have important applications.

The situation can be summarized with the help of a so-called truth table. Let the number 1 stand for "true" and the number 0 stand for "false." The expression xORy returns the value 1 provided either x is true or y is true. Only if *both* x and y are false does xORy return the value 0. This gives rise to the following four equations: $1 + 1 = 1$, $1 + 0 = 1$, $0 + 1 = 1$, and $0 + 0 = 0$. Just as in the case of the AND operator, the situation for the OR operator can be summarized with a truth table where we have used the letters T for true and F for false to emphasize the interpretation we have in mind (see the accompanying illustration).

The latter half of the 19th century saw several further extensions and refinements of Boole's algebra, but Boole's central concepts remained valid. Of special interest was the work of the German mathematician Ernst Schröder (1841–1902), who developed a complete set of axioms for Boolean algebra. (Boole's axioms, listed previously, were incomplete.)

OR	T	F
T	T	T
F	T	F

Truth table for the modern version of the operation OR.

Axioms are a "bare bones" description of a mathematical system in the sense that everything that can be learned about a mathematical system, whether that system is, for example, Boolean algebra or Euclidean geometry, is a logical consequence of the axioms. In this sense mathematicians concern themselves with revealing facts that are, logically speaking, right before their eyes. The axioms always contain all of the information that one can learn about a system. The problem is that the information is not displayed in an obvious way. Any nonobvious statement that can be deduced from a set of axioms is called a theorem. Most mathematicians occupy themselves with deducing new theorems from theorems that have already been proved; this is the art of mathematical discovery. Unfortunately knowing that statement B is, for example, a logical consequence of statement A gives no insight into whether or not statement A is true.

Fortunately there is a final reason why any theorem is true. The ultimate reason that each theorem in a mathematical system is true is that it can be deduced as a logical consequence of the axioms that define the system. The axioms *are* the subject. It is no exaggeration that, mathematically speaking, one can never be completely sure what it is one is studying until a set of axioms that define the subject has been stated. Finally, a logically consistent set of axioms for any branch of mathematics is important because it ensures that it is possible to develop the mathematics in such a way that no statement can be proved both true and false. Placing Boole's algebra on a firmer logical foundation was Schröder's contribution.

In the sense that he axiomatized the Boolean algebra, Schröder completed the subject: He put Boolean algebra into the logical form that we know today. Of course, many new theorems have been proved in the intervening century or so since Schröder's death, but the theorems were proved in the context of Schöder's axioms. Logicians, philosophers, and a few mathematicians were quick to recognize the value of Boole's insights. His ideas provided a conceptual foundation that enabled the user to examine more closely the relationships that exist between logic and mathematics. Many mathematicians, inspired by Boole's work, went on to do just that. This is one implication of Boole's discoveries, but Boolean algebra has had a more immediate impact on our lives through its use in the design of computer circuitry.

Boolean Algebra and Computers

Boole knew nothing about computers, of course. He died 15 years before the invention of the light bulb, and the first

Cray 2 Supercomputer. The microprocessors on which the machine depends would not be possible without Boolean algebra. (Courtesy National Aeronautics and Space Administration)

electronic digital computer began operation in 1946—more than 80 years after his death. Nevertheless the design of computer chips is one of the most important applications of Boolean algebra, because Boole's algebra was deliberately created so that it only used the numbers 0 and 1. Two numerical values are all that is necessary in Boolean algebra, and two digits are all that are necessary to express ideas in binary code. (*Binary code* is a way of coding information that depends on precisely two symbols, which, for convenience, are often represented by the digits 0 and 1.)

To appreciate how this works, we can imagine a computer that performs three functions. First, the computer reads an input file consisting of a string of binary digits. (The input file is the information that the computer has been programmed to process.) Second, the computer processes, or alters, the input file in accordance with some preprogrammed set of instructions. Third, the computer prints the results of these manipulations. This is the output file, which we can imagine as consisting of binary code as well. (Of course, the binary output is usually rewritten in a more user-friendly format, but the details of this reformatting process do not concern us here.) The output file is the reason we buy the computer. It represents the answer, the work performed by the machine on the input file.

The middle step, the processing part of this sequence, is the step in which we are interested. The processing takes place via a set of electronic circuits. By an *electronic circuit* we mean any structure through which electricity can flow. Circuits are manufactured in a variety of sizes and can be made of a variety of materials. What is important is that each circuit is capable of modifying or regulating the flow of electrical current in certain very specific ways. The actual control function of the circuit is affected through a set of switches or *gates*. The gates themselves are easily described in terms of Boolean operators.

There are several types of gates. They either correspond to or can be described in terms of the three common Boolean operators, the AND, OR, and NOT operators. The names of the gates are even derived from Boolean algebra: There are AND-gates, OR-gates, and NOT-gates. By combining Boolean operators we also obtain two other common types of gates: NAND-gates and NOR-gates. Each type of gate regulates the flow of electric current subject to certain conditions.

The idea is that under most conditions there is always a very-low-level current flowing through each circuit. This current is constant and has no effect on whether the gate is "open" or "closed." When, however, the voltage of the input current rises above a certain pre-specified level, the gate is activated. The level of voltage required to activate the gate is called the threshold voltage. Activity occurs whenever the voltage exceeds the threshold level, and activity ceases when the voltage falls below the threshold.

To see how Boolean algebra comes into play, we describe the AND-gate and the OR-gate. An AND-gate has two inputs, just as the Boolean operator AND has two arguments or independent variables. In the case of the AND-gate, we can let x represent the voltage at one input and y represent the voltage at the other input. When the voltage x *and* the voltage y *simultaneously* exceed the threshold voltage, the AND-gate allows current to pass from one side to another. If, however, the voltage in either or both of the inputs falls below the threshold voltage, current does not pass to the other side of the gate. It is in this sense that the AND-gate is a physical representation of Boole's own AND operator. Instead of classes of objects, or binary digits, however, the AND-gate operates on electric current.

Similarly the OR-gate is designed to be inclusive, just as the more modern version of the Boolean operator OR is defined inclusively: If either x or y is true, then xORy is also true. The OR-gate operates on two inputs. We can represent the voltage in one input with the letter x and the voltage in the second input with the letter y. If either x or y is at or above the threshold voltage then the OR-gate allows the current to pass. Otherwise, the current does not pass.

The five switching circuits, AND-, OR-, NOT-, NOR-, and NAND-gates, are combined in often very complex configurations, but the goal is always the same: They modify input in the form of electric current to produce a new electrical current as output. The user interprets the output as specific information, but this is an additional interpretation that is placed on the electrical patterns that emerge from the configuration of circuits. There could be no better physical representation of Boolean algebra than the logic circuits of a computer.

George Boole's exposition of Boolean algebra is contained in a pamphlet, "Mathematical Analysis of Logic" (1847), and a book, *An Investigation into the Laws of Thought on Which are Founded the Mathematical Theories of Logic and Probabilities* (1854). In these works we find not just a new branch of mathematics, but also a new way of thinking about mathematics. Boole's approach was deliberately more abstract than that of his predecessors. This highly abstract approach, far from making his algebra useless, made his algebra one of the most useful of all mathematical innovations. The most important practical applications of Boole's philosophical and mathematical investigations would not be apparent, however, until about a century after "Mathematical Analysis of Logic" was published.

8

THE THEORY OF MATRICES AND DETERMINANTS

Many new types of algebraic structures have been defined and studied since the time of Galois. Today, in addition to groups and fields, mathematicians study algebraic structures called rings, semigroups, and algebras to name a few. (Here *algebra* refers to a particular type of mathematical object.) Each structure is composed of one or more sets of objects on which one or more operations are defined. The *operations* are rules for combining objects in the sets. The sets and operations together form a *structure*, and it is the goal of the mathematician to discover as much as possible about the logical relationships that exist among different parts of the structure.

In this modern approach to algebra the nature of the objects in the set is usually not specified. The objects are represented by letters. The letters may represent numbers, polynomials, or something else entirely, but usually no interpretation is placed on the letters at all. It is only the relationships that exist *between* objects and sets of objects—not the objects and sets themselves—that are of interest to the mathematician.

One of the first and most important of these "new" mathematical structures to receive the attention of mathematicians was the algebra of matrices. Matrices are tables of numbers or symbols. They combine according to some of the same rules that numbers obey, but some of the relationships that exist between matrices are different from the analogous relationships between numbers.

An important part of the theory of matrices is the theory of determinants. Today a determinant is often described as a function of a matrix. For example, if the elements in the matrix are numbers, then—provided the matrix has as many rows as columns—we can often use those elements to compute a number called a determinant. The determinant reveals a great deal of useful information about the (square) matrix. If a matrix represents a system of equations, then the determinant can tell us whether there exists a single solution to the system or whether there are infinitely many solutions. In theory we can even use determinants to compute solutions to systems of equations (although, as we will soon see, the work involved in doing so is usually enormous—too much work to make it a practical approach to problem solving).

The theory of matrices and determinants has proved to be one of the most useful of all branches of mathematics. Not only is the theory an important tool in the solution of many problems within the field of mathematics, it is also one of the most useful of all branches of mathematics in the development of science and engineering. The reason is that this is the type of mathematics that one must know in order to solve systems of linear equations. (A *linear equation* is an equation in which every term is either the product of a number and a variable of the first power or simply a number. For example, $x + y = 1$ is a linear equation, but $x^2 + y = 1$ is not because the x term is raised to the second power.)

Most of us are introduced to systems of linear equations while we are still in junior or senior high school. These are "small" systems, usually involving two or three independent variables. We begin with small systems because the amount of work involved in solving systems of linear equations increases rapidly as the number of variables increases. Unfortunately these small systems fail to convey the tremendous scope of the subject. Today many mathematicians, scientists, and engineers are engaged in solving systems of equations involving many thousands of independent variables. The rush to develop computer algorithms that quickly and accurately solve ever-larger systems of equations has attracted the attention of many mathematicians around the world. The history of matrices, determinants, and related parts of mathematics, however, begins long before the advent of the computer.

Early Ideas

Today when determinants and matrices are taught matrices are introduced first, and determinants are described as functions of matrices. But historically determinants were discovered almost 200 years before mathematicians began to study matrices.

The Japanese mathematician Seki Kōwa, also known as Takakazu (1642–1708), was the first person to discover the idea of a determinant and investigate some of the mathematics associated with this concept. Seki was born into a samurai warrior family, but at an early age he was adopted by a family of the ruling class. When Seki was age nine a family servant who knew mathematics introduced him to the subject. He demonstrated mathematical talent almost immediately, and later in life Seki became known as the Arithmetical Sage. Today he is often described as the founder of Japanese mathematics. This is something of an exaggeration. There was mathematics in Japan before Seki. Nevertheless he was certainly a very important person in the history of Japanese mathematics.

The Arithmetical Sage published very little work during his life. In fact, as was the custom in Japan at the time, he disclosed much of his work to only a select few. As a consequence much of what we know about his discoveries is secondhand or thirdhand. Some scholars attribute a great many accomplishments to him: an (unproved) version of the fundamental theorem of algebra, discoveries in the field of calculus, complex algorithms for discovering solutions to algebraic equations, and more. Other scholars attribute quite a bit less. It is certain, however, that Seki discovered determinants, because his writings on this subject are well known.

Seki's ideas on determinants are fairly complex, and he used them in ways that would be difficult to describe here. A simpler approach to determinants was discovered independently in Europe about 10 years after Seki made his initial discovery. The German mathematician and philosopher Gottfried Leibniz (1646–1716) was the second person to discover what we now call determinants.

Leibniz's life and some of his other contributions to mathematics have already been described elsewhere in this volume. With respect to determinants, Leibniz indicated that he was sometimes required to solve a set of three linear equations involving two variables. Such a system may or may not have a solution. Leibniz discovered that the determinant could be used to establish a criterion for the existence or nonexistence of a solution.

In modern notation we might represent a system of three equations in two unknowns as follows:

$$a_{11} + a_{12}x + a_{13}y = 0$$
$$a_{21} + a_{22}x + a_{23}y = 0$$
$$a_{31} + a_{32}x + a_{33}y = 0$$

The letters a_{ij} represent numbers called coefficients. All the coefficients on the left side of the column of "equals" signs can be viewed as part of a table. In that case the first index—the i-index—indicates the row in which the number appears, and the second index—the j-index—indicates the column. (The coefficient a_{12}, for example, belongs to the first row and the second column.) Notice that the first column contains no variables.

Leibniz's system of equations contains more equations—there are three of them—than there are variables; there are only two variables. When the number of equations exceeds the number of variables, the possibility exists that there are simply too many constraints on the variables and that no values for x and y can simultaneously satisfy all the equations. Mathematicians today call such a system—a system for which there are no solutions—overdetermined. But even when there are more equations than there are variables, it is still possible that solutions exist. What Leibniz discovered is a criterion for determining whether such a system of equations is overdetermined. His criterion is very general, and it does not involve computing the solutions to the equations themselves. Instead it places a constraint on the numbers in the table of coefficients. The key is using the a_{ij} to compute a number that we now call the determinant. Leibniz wrote that when the determinant of this type of system is 0, a solution exists. When the determinant is not 0, there are no values of x and y that can simultaneously satisfy all three equations. In addition Leibniz understood how to use determinants to calculate the values of the variables that would satisfy the system of equations.

Leibniz had made an important discovery: He had found a way to investigate the existence of solutions for an entire class of problems. He did this with a new type of function, the determinant, that depends only on the coefficients appearing in the equations themselves. He described his discoveries in letters to a colleague, but for whatever reason he did not publish these results for a wider audience. In fact Leibniz's ideas were not published for more than 150 years after his death. As a consequence his ideas were not widely known among the mathematicians of his time and had little impact on the development of the subject.

Mathematicians again began to look at determinants as a tool in understanding systems of equations about 50 years after Leibniz first described his discoveries. Initially these ideas were stated and proved only for small systems of variables that in modern notation might be written like this:

$$a_{11}x + a_{12}y + a_{13}z = b_1$$
$$a_{21}x + a_{22}y + a_{23}z = b_2$$
$$a_{31}x + a_{32}y + a_{33}z = b_3$$

The notation is similar to what Leibniz used. The differences are that (1) here there are three equations in three variables and (2) the b_i represent any numbers.

Part of the difficulty that these mathematicians had in applying their insights about determinants to larger systems of equations is that their algebraic notation was not good enough. Determinants can be difficult to describe without very good notation. The calculation of determinants—even for small systems—involves quite a bit of arithmetic, and the algebraic notation needed to describe the procedure can be very complicated as well. For example, the determinant of the system in the previous paragraph is

$$a_{11}a_{22}a_{33} + a_{12}a_{23}a_{31} + a_{13}a_{21}a_{32}$$
$$- a_{31}a_{22}a_{13} - a_{32}a_{23}a_{11} - a_{33}a_{21}a_{12}$$

(The general formula for computing determinants of square matrices of any size is too complicated to describe here. It can, however, be found in any textbook on linear algebra.)

Notice that for a general system of three equations in three unknowns the formula for the 3×3 matrix given in the preceding paragraph involves 17 arithmetic operations, that is, 17 additions, subtractions, and multiplications. Computing the determinant of a general system of four equations and four unknowns involves several times as much work when measured by the number of arithmetic operations involved.

In 1750 the Swiss mathematician Gabriel Cramer (1704–50) published the method now known as Cramer's rule, a method for using determinants to solve any system of n linear equations in n unknowns, where n represents any positive integer greater than 1. Essentially Cramer's rule involves computing multiple determinants. Theoretically it is a very important insight into the relationships between determinants and systems of linear equations. Practically speaking Cramer's rule is of little use, because it requires far too many computations. The idea is simple enough, however. For example, in the system of equations given three paragraphs previous, the solution for each variable can be expressed as a fraction in which the numerator and the denominator are both determinants. The denominator of the fraction is the determinant of the system of equations. The numerator of the fraction is the determinant obtained from the original system of equations by replacing the column of coefficients associated with the variable of interest with the column consisting of (b_1, b_2, b_3). In modern notation we might write the value of x as

$$x = \frac{\begin{vmatrix} b_1 & a_{12} & a_{13} \\ b_2 & a_{22} & a_{23} \\ b_3 & a_{32} & a_{33} \end{vmatrix}}{\begin{vmatrix} a_{11} & a_{12} & a_{13} \\ a_{21} & a_{22} & a_{23} \\ a_{31} & a_{32} & a_{33} \end{vmatrix}}$$

where the vertical lines indicate the determinant of the table of numbers inside. A more computational approach to expressing the value of x looks like this:

$$x = \frac{b_1 a_{22} a_{33} + a_{12} a_{23} b_3 + a_{13} b_2 a_{32} - b_3 a_{22} a_{13} - a_{32} a_{23} b_1 - a_{33} b_2 a_{12}}{a_{11} a_{22} a_{33} + a_{12} a_{23} a_{31} + a_{13} a_{21} a_{32} - a_{31} a_{22} a_{13} - a_{32} a_{23} a_{13} - a_{33} a_{21} a_{12}}$$

Writing out the solution in this way for a system of five equations with five unknowns would take up much of this page.

In the years immediately following the publication of this method of solution, mathematicians expended a great deal of effort seeking easier ways to compute determinants for certain special cases as well as applications for these ideas. These ideas became increasingly important as they found their way into physics.

Spectral Theory

New insights into the mathematics of systems of linear equations arose as mathematicians sought to apply analysis, that branch of mathematics that arose out of the discovery of calculus, to the study of problems in physics. The three mathematicians who pointed the way to these new discoveries were all French: Jean Le Rond d'Alembert (1717–83), Joseph-Louis Lagrange (1736–1813), and Pierre-Simon Laplace (1749–1827). All three mathematicians contributed to the ideas about to be described; of the three d'Alembert was the first.

Jean Le Rond d'Alembert has already been mentioned briefly in this volume in association with the fundamental theorem of algebra. His biological parents were both wealthy and socially prominent. When their child was an infant they abandoned him on the steps of a church called Saint Jean le Ronde, which is the source of most of his name. (He named himself d'Alembert at college.) D'Alembert's biological father eventually found a home for Jean le Ronde with a Parisian family of very modest means named Rousseau. They raised d'Alembert, and d'Alembert considered them his true family. He continued to live with them until he was middle-aged, and when later he achieved prominence as a scientist, he spurned his biological mother's attempts to make contact with him.

D'Alembert's biological father never acknowledged his paternity, but he made sure that his son had sufficient money for a first-rate education. In college d'Alembert studied theology, medicine, and law, but he eventually settled on mathematics. Surprisingly d'Alembert taught himself mathematics while pursuing his other studies, and except for a few private lessons he was entirely self-taught.

Soon after beginning his mathematical studies, d'Alembert distinguished himself as a mathematician, a physicist, and a personality. Never hesitant to criticize the work of others, d'Alembert lived a life marked by almost continuous controversy as well as mathematical and philosophical accomplishments. In his own day d'Alembert was probably best known for his work on a massive encyclopedia that was one of the great works of the Enlightenment.

With respect to systems of linear equations, d'Alembert was interested in developing and solving a set of equations that would represent the motion of a very thin, very light string along which several weights were arrayed. With one end tied to a support, the weighted string is allowed to swing back and forth. Under these conditions the motion of the string is quite irregular. Some mathematicians of the time believed that the motion was too complicated to predict. D'Alembert, however, solved the problem for small motions of the string.

The analytical details of d'Alembert's solution are too complicated to describe here, but the algebra is not. Broadly speaking d'Alembert reduced his problem to what is now known as an eigenvalue problem. A general eigenvalue problem looks like this:

$$a_{11}x + a_{12}y + a_{13}z = \lambda x$$
$$a_{21}x + a_{22}y + a_{23}z = \lambda y$$
$$a_{31}x + a_{32}y + a_{33}z = \lambda z$$

In d'Alembert's problem the unknowns, here represented by the letters x, y, and z, represented functions rather than numbers, but this distinction has no bearing on the algebra that we are interested in discussing.

This system of linear equations is different from the others we have considered in three important ways:

1. The unknowns, x, y, and z, appear on both sides of each equation.

2. The number represented by the Greek letter λ, or lambda, is also an unknown. It is called the eigenvalue of the system of equations.

3. The goal of the mathematician is to find all eigenvalues as well as the solutions for x, y, and z that are associated with each eigenvalue. Each eigenvalue determines a different set of values for x, y, and z.

The problem of determining the eigenvalues associated with each system of equations is important because eigenvalues often have important physical interpretations.

D'Alembert discovered that the only reasonable solutions to his equations were associated with negative eigenvalues. Solutions associated with positive eigenvalues—that is, solutions associated with values of λ greater than 0—were not physically realistic. A solution associated with a positive eigenvalue predicted that once the string was set in motion, the arc along which it swung would become larger and larger instead of slowly "dying down" as actually occurs. The observation that the eigenvalues had interesting physical interpretations was also made by other scientists at about the same time.

Pierre-Simon Laplace and Joseph-Louis Lagrange reached similar sorts of conclusions in their study of the motion of the planets. Their research, as did that of d'Alembert, also generated systems of linear equations, where each unknown represented a function (as opposed to a number). They studied systems of six equations in six unknowns because at the time there were only six known planets. Laplace and Lagrange discovered that solutions associated with positive eigenvalues predicted that small perturbations in planetary motion would become ever larger over time. One consequence of Laplace's and Lagrange's observation is that any solution associated with a positive eigenvalue predicted that over time the solar system would eventually fly apart. Lagrange rejected positive eigenvalues on the basis of physical reasoning: The solar system had not already flown apart. Laplace ruled out the existence of positive eigenvalues associated with his system of equations on mathematical grounds. He proved that in a system in which all the planets moved in the same direction, the eigenvalues must all be negative. He concluded that the solar system is stable—that is, that it would not fly apart over time.

Notice the similarities between the model of the solar system and the weighted string problem of d'Alembert. In each case solutions associated with positive eigenvalues were shown to be "nonphysical" in the sense that they did not occur in nature. The connection between algebraic ideas (eigenvalues) and physical ones (weighted strings and planetary orbits) spurred further research into both.

To convey the flavor of the type of insights that Lagrange and Laplace were pursuing, consider the following eigenvalue problem taken from one of the preceding paragraphs. It is reproduced again here for ease of reference.

$$a_{11}x + a_{12}y + a_{13}z = \lambda x$$
$$a_{21}x + a_{22}y + a_{23}z = \lambda y$$
$$a_{31}x + a_{32}y + a_{33}z = \lambda z$$

Notice that we can subtract away each term on the right from both sides of each equation. The result is

$$(a_{11} - \lambda)x + a_{12}y + a_{13}z = 0$$
$$a_{21}x + (a_{22} - \lambda)y + a_{23}z = 0$$
$$a_{31}x + a_{32}y + (a_{33} - \lambda)z = 0$$

This is a new set of coefficients. The coefficient in the upper left corner is now $a_{11} - \lambda$ instead of simply a_{11}. The middle coefficient is now $a_{22} - \lambda$ instead of a_{22}, and similarly the coefficient in the lower right corner is now $a_{33} - \lambda$ instead of a_{33}. The other coefficients are unchanged. From this new set of coefficients a new determinant can be computed. (We can, in fact, use the formula already given for 3 × 3-matrices on page 157: Simply substitute $a_{11} - \lambda$, $a_{22} - \lambda$, $a_{33} - \lambda$ for a_{11}, a_{22}, and a_{33} in the formula.) The result is a third-degree polynomial in the variable λ. This polynomial is called the characteristic polynomial, and its roots are exactly the eigenvalues of the original system of linear equations.

The discovery of the characteristic polynomial established an important connection between two very important branches of algebra: the theory of determinants and the theory of algebraic equations. Laplace and Legendre had discovered the results for particular systems of equations, but there was as yet no general theory of either determinants or eigenvalues. Their work, however, pointed to complex and interesting connections among the theory of determinants, the theory of algebraic equations, and physics. This very rich interplay of different areas of mathematics and science is such a frequent feature of discovery in both fields that today we sometimes take it for granted. At the time of Laplace and Legendre, however, the existence of these interconnections was a discovery in itself.

The work of d'Alembert, Laplace, and Legendre gave a great impetus to the study of eigenvalue problems. Investigators wanted to understand the relationships that existed between the coefficients in the equations and the eigenvalues. They wanted to know how many eigenvalues were associated with each set of equations. The result of these inquiries was the beginning of a branch of mathematics called spectral theory—the eigenvalues are sometimes called the spectral values of the system—and the pioneer in the theoretical study of these types of questions was the French mathematician Augustin-Louis Cauchy (1789–1857).

Cauchy was born at a time when France was very politically unstable. This instability profoundly affected both his personal and his professional life. First the French Revolution of 1789 occurred. While Cauchy was still a boy, the revolution was supplanted by a period called the Reign of Terror (1793–94), a period when approximately 17,000 French citizens were executed and many more were imprisoned. In search of safety, Cauchy's family fled Paris, the city of his birth, to a village called Arcueil. It was in Arcueil that Cauchy first met Laplace. Lagrange and Laplace were friends of Cauchy's father, and Lagrange advised the elder Cauchy that his son could best prepare himself for mathematics by studying languages. Dutifully Cauchy studied languages for two years before beginning his study of mathematics.

By the age of 21 Cauchy was working as a military engineer—at this time Napoléon was leading wars against his European neighbors—and pursuing research in mathematics in his spare time. Cauchy wanted to work in an academic environment, but this goal proved difficult for him. He was passed over for appointments by several colleges and worked briefly at others. He eventually secured a position at the Académie des Sciences in 1816. There he replaced the distinguished professor of geometry Gaspard Monge, who lost the position for political reasons.

In July of 1830 there was another revolution in France. This time King Charles X was replaced by Louis-Philippe. As a condition of employment Cauchy was required to swear an oath of allegiance to the new king, but this he refused to do. The result was that he lost the academic post that had meant so much to him. Cauchy found a position in Turin, Italy, and later in Prague in what is now the Czech Republic. By 1838 he was able to return to his old position in Paris as a researcher but not as a teacher: The requirement of the oath was still in effect, and Cauchy still refused to swear his allegiance. It was not until 1848, when Louis-Philippe was overthrown, that Cauchy, who never did swear allegiance, was able to teach again.

All biographies of Cauchy indicate that he was a difficult man, brusque and preachy. As a consequence he often did not obtain academic appointments that he very much desired. This pattern proved a source of frustration throughout his life. Even toward the end of his career, after producing one of the largest and most creative bodies of work in the history of mathematics, he still failed to gain an appointment that he sought at the Collège de France.

Today there are theorems and problems in many branches of mathematics that bear Cauchy's name. His ideas are fundamental to the fields of analysis, group theory, and geometry as well as spectral theory. After his death his papers were collected and published. They fill 27 volumes.

One of Cauchy's earliest papers was about the theory of determinants. He revisited the problems associated with determinants and eigenvalues several times during his life, each time adding something different. We concentrate on two of his contributions, which we sometimes express in a more modern and convenient notation than Cauchy used.

Cauchy wrote determinants as tables of numbers. For example, he would write the determinant of the system of linear equations

$$a_{11}x + a_{12}y + a_{13}z = b_1$$
$$a_{21}x + a_{22}y + a_{23}z = b_2$$
$$a_{31}x + a_{32}y + a_{33}z = b_3$$

as the table of numbers

$$a_{11}\ a_{12}\ a_{13}$$
$$a_{21}\ a_{22}\ a_{23}$$
$$a_{31}\ a_{32}\ a_{33}$$

The coefficients a_{11}, a_{22}, a_{33} lie along what is called the main diagonal. Cauchy proved that when all the numbers in the table are real and when the table itself is symmetric with respect to the main diagonal—so that, for example, $a_{12} = a_{21}$—the eigenvalues, or roots of the characteristic equation, are real numbers. This was the first such observation relating the eigenvalues of the equations to the structure of the table of numbers from which the determinant is calculated. Part of the value of this observation is that it enables the user to describe various properties of the eigenvalues without actually computing them. (As a practical matter, computing eigenvalues for large systems of equations involves a great deal of work.)

Cauchy also discovered a kind of "determinant arithmetic." In modern language he discovered that when two matrices are multiplied together in a certain way, the determinant of the product matrix is the product of the determinants of the two matrices. In other words, if A and B are two square arrays of numbers, then

$\det(A \times B) = \det(A) \times \det(B)$, where $\det(A)$ is shorthand for "the determinant of A." These theorems are important because they hint at the existence of a deeper logical structure.

Another very important discovery by Cauchy is that the roots of the characteristic polynomial are invariant. Invariance is a concept that is very important in many branches of mathematics. For example, in geometry, when a triangle is moved from one part of the plane to another or when it is rotated about a point, the size and shape of the triangle are unchanged. We say that under these types of motions, the size and shape of the triangle are invariant. Mathematicians find the idea of invariance helpful, because it can be used to help determine when two things—for example, two systems of linear equations or two triangles—that may look very different are in some sense the same.

A set of equations can be imagined as a kind of description. They describe a set of numbers—the numbers that satisfy the equations. Different-looking descriptions (equations) can sometimes represent solutions that are, if not identical, then at least similar. Giving a precise meaning to these very general statements requires mathematicians to identify those properties of the system that are fundamental or *invariant*. The coefficients that appear in a system of linear equations, for example, are not fundamental, since we could obtain all of the same solutions after multiplying both sides of every equation by any number other than 0. On the other hand, the eigenvalues, or roots of the characteristic equation, are an early example of a fundamental or invariant property of the system. Cauchy's insights into these matters form an important part of the foundations of spectral theory.

The Theory of Matrices

Credit for founding the theory of matrices is often given to the English mathematician Arthur Cayley (1821–95) and his close friend the English mathematician James Joseph Sylvester (1814–97), but others had essentially the same ideas at roughly the same time. The German mathematicians Ferdinand Georg Frobenius (1849–1917) and Ferdinand Gotthold Max Eisenstein

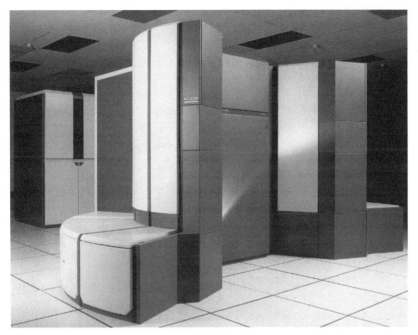

Cray Y 190A Supercomputer. Much of the software used by the machine to solve computationally intensive problems in aeronautics is expressed in terms of matrix algebra, an application of their work that 19th-century mathematicians could not have anticipated. (Courtesy of the National Aeronautics and Space Administration)

(1823–52) and the French mathematician Charles Hermite (1822–1901) are three mathematicians who also made discoveries similar to those of Cayley and Sylvester. Eisenstein, in fact, seems to have been the first to think of developing an algebra of matrices. He had been studying systems of linear equations of the form

$$a_{11}x + a_{12}y + a_{13}z = b_1$$
$$a_{21}x + a_{22}y + a_{23}z = b_2$$
$$a_{31}x + a_{32}y + a_{33}z = b_3$$

and began to consider the possibility of analyzing the mathematical properties of what is essentially the "skeleton" of the equation, the table of coefficients that today we would write as

$$\begin{bmatrix} a_{11}\ a_{12}\ a_{13} \\ a_{21}\ a_{22}\ a_{23} \\ a_{31}\ a_{32}\ a_{33} \end{bmatrix}$$

Although this idea may seem similar to that of Cauchy's tables of coefficients, it is not. It is true that Cauchy used tables of numbers, but he used them as an alternate way of representing the determinant function. Eisenstein contemplated the possibility of developing an algebra in which the objects of interest were not numbers, or the determinant function, or even polynomials, but rather matrices. Unfortunately he died before he could follow up on these ideas. In this discussion we follow the usual practice of emphasizing Cayley's and Sylvester's contributions, but it would, for example, be possible to describe the history of matrix algebra from the point of view of Frobenius, Eisenstein, and Hermite as well.

A great deal has been written about Cayley and Sylvester as researchers and as friends. Each distinguished himself in mathematics at university, Cayley at Trinity College, Cambridge, and Sylvester at Saint John's College, Cambridge. Cayley's early academic successes led to increased opportunities at college as well as a stipend. Sylvester's early successes proved to be a source of frustration. He was barred from a number of opportunities because of his faith—he was Jewish—and he left Saint John's without graduating. He would eventually receive his degrees in 1841 from Trinity College, Dublin.

When it came time to find employment as mathematicians, neither Cayley nor Sylvester found much in the way of work. Cayley solved the problem by becoming a lawyer. Sylvester, too, became a lawyer, but his route to the legal profession was more circuitous. In 1841 he left Great Britain and worked briefly on the faculty at the University of Virginia. He left the university several months later after an altercation with a student. Unable to find another position in the United States, he returned to London in 1843 to work as an actuary. While working as an actuary, Sylvester tutored private pupils in mathematics, and it was during this time that he tutored the medical pioneer Florence Nightingale in mathematics. (Nightingale was a firm and early believer in the use of statistics to evaluate medical protocols.) Finally, in 1850 Sylvester, as did Cayley, turned to the legal profession to earn a living. That same year while they were both working as lawyers Cayley and Sylvester met and formed a lifelong friendship.

Cayley worked as a lawyer for 14 years before he joined the faculty at Cambridge in 1863. Sylvester worked as a lawyer for five years until he found a position at the Royal Military Academy, Woolwich. Cayley, a contemplative man, remained at Cambridge for most of the rest of his working life. The exception occurred when he spent a year at Johns Hopkins University in Baltimore, Maryland, at Sylvester's invitation. By contrast Sylvester remained at Woolwich for 15 years and then, in 1876, moved back to the United States to work at Johns Hopkins University. (Sylvester played an important role in establishing advanced mathematical research in the United States.) In 1883 Sylvester returned to the United Kingdom to work at Oxford University.

Although they were both creative mathematicians their approaches to mathematics were quite different. Cayley spoke carefully and produced mathematical papers that were well reasoned and rigorous. By contrast, Sylvester was excitable and talkative and did not hesitate to substitute his intuition for a rigorous proof. He sometimes produced mathematical papers that contained a great deal of elegant and poetic description but were decidedly short on mathematical rigor. Nevertheless his intuition could usually be shown to be correct.

The theory of determinants, spectral theory, and the theory of linear equations had already revealed many of the basic properties of matrices before anyone conceived of the idea of a matrix. Arthur Cayley remarked that logically the theory of matrices precedes the theory of determinants, but historically these theories were developed in just the opposite order. It was Cayley, author of "A Memoir on the Theory of Matrices," published in 1858, who first described the properties of matrices as mathematical objects. He had been studying systems of equations of the form

$$a_{11}x + a_{12}y = u$$
$$a_{21}x + a_{22}y = v$$

(Notice that in this set of equations the variables x and y are the independent variables and the variables u and v are the dependent variables.) Apparently in an effort to streamline his notation he simply wrote $\begin{bmatrix} a_{11} & a_{12} \\ a_{21} & a_{22} \end{bmatrix}$, a shorthand form of the same equation that preserves all of the information.

Having defined a matrix he began to study the set of all such matrices as a mathematical system. The most useful and richest part of the theory concerns the mathematical properties of square matrices of a fixed size—they are called the set of all $n \times n$ matrices, where n represents a fixed natural number greater than 1. In what follows we restrict our attention to 2×2 matrices for simplicity, but similar definitions and results exist for square matrices of any size.

Matrix addition is defined elementwise. Given a pair of 2×2 matrices, which we can represent with the symbols $\begin{bmatrix} a_{11} & a_{12} \\ a_{21} & a_{22} \end{bmatrix}$ and $\begin{bmatrix} b_{11} & b_{12} \\ b_{21} & b_{22} \end{bmatrix}$, the sum of these two matrices is $\begin{bmatrix} a_{11} + b_{11} & a_{12} + b_{12} \\ a_{21} + b_{21} & a_{22} + b_{22} \end{bmatrix}$.

(The difference of the two matrices is simply obtained by writing a subtraction sign in place of the addition sign.) With this definition of matrix addition the matrix $\begin{bmatrix} 0 & 0 \\ 0 & 0 \end{bmatrix}$ plays the same role as the number 0 in the real number system.

Cayley also defined matrix multiplication. The definition of matrix multiplication is not especially obvious to most of us, but to Cayley it was a simple matter because he and others had used this definition in the study of other mathematics problems, even before he had begun the study of matrices (see Matrix Multiplication).

There are differences, of course, between matrix arithmetic and the arithmetic of numbers that we learn in grade school. One significant difference is that multiplication is not commutative: That is, the order in which we multiply two matrices makes a difference. Given two matrices, which we represent with the letters A and B, it is generally false that AB and BA are equal. Ordinary multiplication of numbers, by contrast, is commutative: 3×4 and 4×3, for example, represent the same number.

Another significant difference between matrix multiplication and ordinary multiplication is that (except 0) every *number* has a multiplicative inverse. In other words, if the letter x represents any number other than 0, there is another number—which we can write as x^{-1}—such that $x \times x^{-1} = 1$. Many matrices, however, have no multiplicative inverse; given a square matrix A, it is often the case that no matrix A^{-1} exists with the property that $A^{-1} A = I$, where I represents the identity matrix—the matrix with 1s along the main diagonal and 0s elsewhere.

There is an additional operation that one can perform in matrix arithmetic that connects the theory of matrices with ordinary numbers: Not only can one compute the product of two $n \times n$ matrices; it is also possible to multiply any matrix by a number. For example, if the letter c represents any number then the product of c and the matrix $\begin{bmatrix} a_{11} & a_{12} \\ a_{21} & a_{22} \end{bmatrix}$ is $\begin{bmatrix} ca_{11} & ca_{12} \\ ca_{21} & ca_{22} \end{bmatrix}$.

Cayley also investigated polynomials in which the variables that appear in the polynomial represent matrices instead of numbers. His most famous result is the relationship between a square matrix and its characteristic polynomial. On page 163 we described the characteristic polynomial of a matrix. Cayley showed that if the matrix is written in place of the variable in the characteristic polynomial and the indicated operations are performed, the result is always the 0 matrix. In other words, each matrix satisfies the equation obtained by setting its characteristic polynomial to 0, so it is sometimes said that every matrix is a root of its own characteristic polynomial. This is called the Hamilton–Cayley theorem after Cayley and the Irish mathematician and astronomer Sir William Henry Rowan Hamilton (1805–65), who discovered the same theorem but from a different point of view.

Cayley was a prominent and prolific mathematician, but his work on matrices did not attract much attention inside Great Britain. Outside Great Britain it was unknown. Consequently many of his ideas were later rediscovered elsewhere. In the 1880s James Joseph Sylvester, who in the intervening years had become one of the most prominent mathematicians of his time, turned his attention to the same questions that Cayley had addressed about

MATRIX MULTIPLICATION

Matrix multiplication is defined for square matrices of a fixed but arbitrary size in such a manner that many of the laws that govern the arithmetic of ordinary numbers carry over to the matrix case. In what follows we restrict our attention to 2×2 matrices, but similar definitions apply to any $n \times n$ matrix.

Let the matrix $\begin{bmatrix} c_{11} & c_{12} \\ c_{21} & c_{22} \end{bmatrix}$ represent the product of the matrices $\begin{bmatrix} a_{11} & a_{12} \\ a_{21} & a_{22} \end{bmatrix}$

and $\begin{bmatrix} b_{11} & b_{12} \\ b_{21} & b_{22} \end{bmatrix}$. Each number c_{ij} is obtained by combining the ith row of

the "a-matrix" with the jth column of the "b-matrix" in the following way:

$$\begin{bmatrix} a_{11} & a_{12} \\ a_{21} & a_{22} \end{bmatrix} \times \begin{bmatrix} b_{11} & b_{12} \\ b_{21} & b_{22} \end{bmatrix} = \begin{bmatrix} a_{11}b_{11} + a_{12}b_{21} & a_{11}b_{12} + a_{12}b_{22} \\ a_{21}b_{11} + a_{22}b_{21} & a_{21}b_{21} + a_{22}b_{22} \end{bmatrix}$$

For example, to compute c_{12}, which is equal to $a_{11}b_{12} + a_{12}b_{22}$, multiply the first entry of the first row of the a-matrix by the first entry of the second column of the b-matrix, then add this to the product of the second entry of the first row of the a-matrix multiplied by the second entry of the second column of the b-matrix. Here are some consequences of this definition of multiplication:

1. The matrix $\begin{bmatrix} 1 & 0 \\ 0 & 1 \end{bmatrix}$ plays the same role as the number 1 in the real number system.

2. If we let A, B, and C represent any three $n \times n$ matrices, then multiplication "distributes" over addition, just as in ordinary arithmetic: $A(B + C) = AB + AC$.

3. If we let A, B, and C represent any three $n \times n$ matrices, the associative property applies: $A(BC) = (AB)C$.

4. Matrix multiplication is not usually commutative: $AB \neq BA$.

three decades earlier. Whether Sylvester had read Cayley's old monograph or rediscovered these ideas independently is not clear. In any case Sylvester's work had the effect of drawing attention to Cayley's earlier discoveries—a fact that seemed to please Sylvester. He always spoke highly of his friend—he once described Cayley's

How did this definition of multiplication arise? Mathematicians, Cayley among them, had already studied functions of the form $y = \dfrac{a_{11}x + a_{12}}{a_{21}x + a_{22}}$. If we take a second function of the same form, say, $z = \dfrac{b_{11}y + b_{12}}{b_{21}y + b_{22}}$, and we write $y = \dfrac{a_{11}x + a_{12}}{a_{21}x + a_{22}}$ in place of y in the expression for z, and finally perform all of the arithmetic, we obtain the following expression:

$$z = \frac{(a_{11}b_{11} + a_{12}b_{21})x + (a_{11}b_{12} + a_{12}b_{22})}{(a_{21}b_{11} + a_{22}b_{21})x + (a_{21}b_{21} + a_{22}b_{22})}.$$ Compare this with the entries in the product matrix already given. The corresponding entries are identical. It is in this sense that matrix multiplication was discovered before matrices were discovered!

memoir on matrices as "the foundation stone" of the subject—but in this case Sylvester's prominence and his emphasis on the contributions of Cayley had the effect of obscuring the work of Frobenius, Eisenstein, Hermite, and others.

Sylvester did more than rediscover Cayley's work, however. Sylvester had made important contributions to the theory of determinants for decades, and he had learned how to use determinants to investigate a number of problems. In a sense he had become familiar with many of the problems that are important to the theory of matrices before discovering matrices themselves. (Sylvester himself coined the term *matrix*.)

Sylvester was interested in the relationships that exist between a matrix and its eigenvalues. He discovered, for example, that if A represents an $n \times n$ matrix and λ is an eigenvalue of A, then λ^j is an eigenvalue of the matrix A^j, where A^j represents the matrix product of A multiplied by itself j times. He produced other results in a similar vein. For example, suppose the matrix A has an inverse. Let A^{-1}, represent the inverse of the matrix A so that $A^{-1} \times A$ equals the *identity matrix*, that is, the matrix with 1s down the main diagonal and 0s elsewhere. Let λ represent an eigenvalue of A; then

James Joseph Sylvester. He helped develop the theory of matrices. (Bettmann/CORBIS)

λ^{-1}—also written as $1/\lambda$—is an eigenvalue of A^{-1}.

The work of Cayley, Sylvester, and others led to the development of a branch of mathematics that proved to be very useful in ways that they could not possibly have predicted. For example, in the early years of the 20th century, physicists were searching for a way of mathematically expressing new ideas about the inner workings of the atom. These were the early years of that branch of physics called quantum mechanics. It turned out that the theory of matrices—developed by Cayley, Sylvester, Frobenius, Hermite, and Eisenstein in the preceding century—was exactly the right language for expressing the ideas of quantum mechanics. All the physicists needed to do was use the mathematics that had been previously developed (see A Computational Application of Matrix Algebra). The theory of matrices proved useful in other ways as well. (Matrices in Ring Theory describes one such area.)

Probably more than any other mathematical discipline, algebra has evolved. Four thousand years ago it was used to facilitate simple computations, painstakingly pressed into clay tablets and left to dry in the desert sun; it is now the language used to frame and solve many of the most computationally complex problems in modern physics and engineering. But algebra is more than a language of scientific computation. Boolean algebra, for example, makes possible the design of logic circuits that enable computers to carry out sophisticated computations. Modern algebra has also enabled mathematicians to see below the surface of mathematics. With the help of the theories of groups, rings, and fields, mathematicians now understand many

A COMPUTATIONAL APPLICATION OF MATRIX ALGEBRA

The interior of the submarine USS Seawolf. (U.S. Navy photo used with permission)

Although we have come to think of computers as "fast" in the sense that they can perform many calculations each second, the truth is that they are not nearly fast enough for scientists and mathematicians interested in fluid dynamics, biochemistry, and geophysics, to name a few branches of science and engineering that depend on large-scale computations. The needs of these scientists and mathematicians drive the development of ever more efficient hardware and software. Engineers are continually designing and building faster computers. Mathematicians are continually devising software that makes more efficient use of the machines available. No sooner are the new software and hardware finished, however, than scientists and mathematicians have imagined even larger, more complicated problems to solve.

Matrix algebra is an integral part of the programs used in numerical analysis, the branch of mathematics devoted to the study of how to use

(continues)

A COMPUTATIONAL APPLICATION OF MATRIX ALGEBRA
(continued)

computers to solve problems in mathematics. A nice example of the use of matrix algebra to solve a computationally intensive problem in real time arises in submarine navigation.

Nuclear submarines are completely dependent on mathematics and computer technology to solve very large sets of algebraic equations. Nuclear submarines are huge ships. They can dive deep and they can cruise underwater at freeway speeds, but they have no windows. The crew inside cannot see outside. Despite the fact that they sail blindly, submarines are nevertheless required sometimes to cruise through waters where they are surrounded by unseen hazards. These hazards include mountains, icebergs projecting deep beneath the surface of the water, and, possibly, other ships and submarines. To navigate through this maze the ship is equipped with sensors that continually collect vast amounts of data about the environment. The raw or unanalyzed data are not in themselves sufficient to enable the crew to navigate. Instead these data serve as input for very large systems of linear equations. The matrices that represent these equations may have hundreds of thousands of entries, each of which represents a coefficient in a very large system of equations. Onboard computers continually solve these very large sets of linear, algebraic equations. The solutions so obtained are interpreted as information about in-the-area ships, icebergs, or undersea mountains. This process of analyzing data through the use of algebraic equations is continuous while the ship is at sea.

The techniques required to manipulate very large matrices are constantly evolving as scientists and engineers seek to solve ever-larger, more complex problems. There is no end in sight. Progress in a variety of scientific and engineering disciplines depends on deeper insight into the algebra of matrices.

of the deeper logical structures and relations on which so much of their subject depends. These insights have contributed to progress in all branches of mathematics. In addition, the symbolic language that previous generations of mathematicians developed to express their algebraic ideas has become the common language of mathematicians, engineers, and scientists the

MATRICES IN RING THEORY

In the 20th century, mathematicians began to investigate a new type of structure called a ring. A ring is a set of elements that can be combined through an operation that is analogous to addition in the following ways:

1. If a and b are elements of the ring, so is $a + b$.
2. Addition is associative: That is, if a, b, and c belong to the ring, then $a + (b + c) = (a + b) + c$.
3. There is an element in the ring analogous to 0—it is even called 0—with the property that $0 + a = a$ for every element a in the ring.
4. For every element a in the ring there is another element called $-a$ that also belongs to the ring such that $a + -a = 0$.
5. $a + b = b + a$ for all a and b in the ring.

There is a second operation defined on the elements in the ring that is somewhat analogous to multiplication. It has the following two properties:

1. If a and b belong to the ring then so does the product ab.
2. If a, b, and c belong to the ring then the associative property holds: $a(bc) = (ab)c$.

Ring multiplication is not usually commutative (so that it is usually false that $ab = ba$), and not every element in the ring has a multiplicative inverse. If this seems familiar, it is because various sets of $n \times n$ matrices together with the operations described in this chapter can be chosen so as to form concrete examples of rings.

The study of the structure of rings became very important during the first third of the 20th century as a result of the work of the German mathematician Emmy Noether (1882–1935). Ring theory is usually fairly abstract. Many mathematicians interested in ring theory often just use letters to represent elements in rings, but matrices are so well understood and have so many fruitful interpretations that it is sometimes helpful to represent a particular ring as a collection of $n \times n$ matrices. These types of matrix representations enable mathematicians to make some of their insights "concrete," even computable, and they enable scientists to make use of the highly abstract musings of the mathematical theorist. The representation of rings and groups via sets of matrices has become an important part of contemporary mathematics, physics, and theoretical chemistry.

world over. Many of the ideas that are central to these diverse and highly mathematical disciplines probably could no longer be expressed without algebra. It is no exaggeration to say that algebra has become the language of mathematics even as mathematics has become the language of science. Algebra is everywhere. It has become indispensable to our way of life.

CHRONOLOGY

ca. 3000 B.C.E.
Hieroglyphic numerals are in use in Egypt.

ca. 2500 B.C.E.
Construction of the Great Pyramid of Khufu takes place.

ca. 2400 B.C.E.
An almost complete system of positional notation is in use in Mesopotamia.

ca. 1800 B.C.E.
The Code of Hammurabi is promulgated.

ca. 1650 B.C.E.
The Egyptian scribe Ahmes copies what is now known as the Ahmes (or Rhind) papyrus from an earlier version of the same document.

ca. 1200 B.C.E.
The Trojan War is fought.

ca. 740 B.C.E.
Homer composes the *Odyssey* and the *Iliad*, his epic poems about the Trojan War.

ca. 585 B.C.E.
Thales of Miletus carries out his research into geometry, marking the beginning of mathematics as a deductive science.

ca. 540 B.C.E.
Pythagoras of Samos establishes the Pythagorean school of philosophy.

ca. 500 B.C.E.
Rod numerals are in use in China.

ca. 420 B.C.E.

Zeno of Elea proposes his philosophical paradoxes.

ca. 399 B.C.E.

Socrates dies.

ca. 360 B.C.E.

Eudoxus, author of the method of exhaustion, carries out his research into mathematics.

ca. 350 B.C.E.

The Greek mathematician Menaechmus writes an important work on conic sections.

ca. 347 B.C.E.

Plato dies.

332 B.C.E.

Alexandria, Egypt, center of Greek mathematics, is founded.

ca. 300 B.C.E.

Euclid of Alexandria writes *Elements*, one of the most influential mathematics books of all time.

ca. 260 B.C.E.

Aristarchus of Samos discovers a method for computing the ratio of the Earth–Moon distance to the Earth–Sun distance.

ca. 230 B.C.E.

Eratosthenes of Cyrene computes the circumference of Earth.

Apollonius of Perga writes *Conics*.

Archimedes of Syracuse writes *The Method*, *Equilibrium of Planes*, and other works.

206 B.C.E.

The Han dynasty is established; Chinese mathematics flourishes.

ca. A.D. 150

Ptolemy of Alexandria writes *Almagest*, the most influential astronomy text of antiquity.

ca. A.D. 250
Diophantus of Alexandria writes *Arithmetica*, an important step forward for algebra.

ca. 320
Pappus of Alexandria writes his *Collection*, one of the last influential Greek mathematical treatises.

415
The death of the Alexandrian philosopher and mathematician Hypatia marks the end of the Greek mathematical tradition.

ca. 476
The astronomer and mathematician Aryabhata is born; Indian mathematics flourishes.

ca. 630
The Hindu mathematician and astronomer Brahmagupta writes *Brahma-sphuta-siddhānta*, which contains a description of place-value notation.

641
The Library of Alexandria is burned.

ca. 775
Scholars in Baghdad begin to translate Hindu and Greek works into Arabic.

ca. 830
Mohammed ibn-Mūsā al-Khwārizmī writes *Hisāb al-jabr wa'l muqābala*, a new approach to algebra.

833
Al-Ma'mūn, founder of the House of Wisdom in Baghdad (now Iraq), dies.

ca. 840
The Jainist mathematician Mahavira writes *Ganita Sara Samgraha*, an important mathematical textbook.

1071
William the Conqueror quells the last of the English rebellions.

1086

An intensive survey of the wealth of England is carried out and summarized in the tables and lists of the *Domesday Book*.

1123

Omar Khayyám, author of *Al-jabr w'al muqābala* and the *Rubáiyát*, the last great classical Islamic mathematician, dies.

ca. 1144

Bhaskara II writes the *Lilavati* and the *Vija-Ganita*, two of the last great works in the classical Indian mathematical tradition.

ca. 1202

Leonardo of Pisa (Fibonacci), author of *Liber Abaci*, arrives in Europe.

1360

Nicholas Oresme, French mathematician and Roman Catholic bishop, represents distance as the area beneath a velocity line.

1471

The German artist Albrecht Dürer is born.

1482

Leonardo da Vinci begins to keep his diaries.

ca. 1541

Niccolò Fontana, an Italian mathematician, also known as Tartaglia, discovers a general method for factoring third-degree algebraic equations.

1543

Copernicus publishes *De Revolutionibus*, marking the start of the Copernican revolution.

1545

Girolamo Cardano, an Italian mathematician and physician, publishes *Ars Magna*, marking the beginning of modern algebra. Later he publishes *Liber de Ludo Aleae*, the first book on probability.

ca. 1554

Sir Walter Raleigh, an explorer, adventurer, amateur mathematician, and patron of the mathematician Thomas Harriot, is born.

1579

François Viète, a French mathematician, publishes *Canon Mathematicus*, marking the beginning of modern algebraic notation.

1585

The Dutch mathematician and engineer Simon Stevin publishes "La disme."

1609

Johannes Kepler, author of Kepler's laws of planetary motion, publishes *Astronomia Nova*.

Galileo Galilei begins his astronomical observations.

1621

The English mathematician and astronomer Thomas Harriot dies. His only work, *Artis Analyticae Praxis*, is published in 1631.

ca. 1630

The French lawyer and mathematician Pierre de Fermat begins a lifetime of mathematical research. He is the first person to claim to have proved "Fermat's last theorem."

1636

Gérard (or Girard) Desargues, a French mathematician and engineer, publishes *Traité de la section perspective*, which marks the beginning of projective geometry.

1637

René Descartes, a French philosopher and mathematician, publishes *Discours de la méthode*, permanently changing both algebra and geometry.

1638

Galileo Galilei publishes *Dialogues Concerning Two New Sciences* while under arrest.

1640

Blaise Pascal, a French philosopher, scientist, and mathematician, publishes *Essai sur les coniques*, an extension of the work of Desargues.

1642

Blaise Pascal manufactures an early mechanical calculator, the Pascaline.

1648

The Thirty Years' War, a series of conflicts that involves much of Europe, ends.

1649

Oliver Cromwell takes control of the English government after a civil war.

1654

Pierre de Fermat and Blaise Pascal exchange a series of letters about probability, thereby inspiring many mathematicians to study the subject.

1655

John Wallis, an English mathematician and clergyman, publishes *Arithmetica Infinitorum*, an important work that presages calculus.

1657

Christian Huygens, a Dutch mathematician, astronomer, and physicist, publishes *De Ratiociniis in Ludo Aleae*, a highly influential text in probability theory.

1662

John Graunt, an English businessman and a pioneer in statistics, publishes his research on the London Bills of Mortality.

1673

Gottfried Leibniz, a German philosopher and mathematician, constructs a mechanical calculator that can perform addition, subtraction, multiplication, division, and extraction of roots.

1683

Seki Kōwa, a Japanese mathematician, discovers the theory of determinants.

1684

Gottfried Leibniz publishes the first paper on calculus, *Nova Methodus pro Maximis et Minimis*.

1687

Isaac Newton, a British mathematician and physicist, publishes *Philosophiae Naturalis Principia Mathematica*, beginning a new era in science.

1693

Edmund Halley, a British mathematician and astronomer, undertakes a statistical study of the mortality statistics in Breslau, Germany.

1698

Thomas Savery, an English engineer and inventor, patents the first steam engine.

1705

Jacob Bernoulli, a Swiss mathematician, dies. His major work on probability, *Ars Conjectandi*, is published in 1713.

1712

The first Newcomen steam engine is installed.

1718

Abraham de Moivre, a French mathematician, publishes *The Doctrine of Chances*, the most advanced text of the time on the theory of probability.

1743

The Anglo-Irish Anglican bishop and philosopher George Berkeley publishes *The Analyst*, an attack on the new mathematics pioneered by Isaac Newton and Gottfried Leibniz.

The French mathematician and philosopher Jean Le Rond d'Alembert begins work on the *Encyclopédie*, one of the great works of the Enlightenment.

1748

Leonhard Euler, a Swiss mathematician, publishes his *Introductio*.

1749

The French mathematician and scientist George-Louis Leclerc Buffon publishes the first volume of *Histoire naturelle*.

1750

Gabriel Cramer, a Swiss mathematician, publishes "Cramer's Rule," a procedure for solving systems of linear equations.

1760

Daniel Bernoulli, a Swiss mathematician and scientist, publishes his probabilistic analysis of the risks and benefits of variolation against smallpox.

1761

Thomas Bayes, an English theologian and mathematician, dies. His "Essay Towards Solving a Problem in the Doctrine of Chances" is published two years later.

The English scientist Joseph Black proposes the idea of latent heat.

1762

Catherine II (Catherine the Great) is proclaimed empress of Russia.

1769

James Watt obtains his first steam engine patent.

1775

American colonists and British troops fight battles at Lexington and Concord, Massachusetts.

1778

Voltaire (François-Marie Arouet), a French writer and philosopher, dies.

1781

William Herschel, a German-born British musician and astronomer, discovers Uranus.

1789

Unrest in France culminates in the French Revolution

1793

The Reign of Terror, a period of brutal, state-sanctioned repression, begins in France.

1794
The French mathematician Adrien-Marie Legendre (or Le Gendre) publishes his *Éléments de géométrie*, a text that influences mathematics education for decades.

Antoine-Laurent Lavoisier, a French scientist and discoverer of the law of conservation of matter, is executed by the French government.

1798
Benjamin Thompson (Count Rumford), a British physicist, proposes the equivalence of heat and work.

1799
Napoléon Bonaparte seizes control of the French government.

Caspar Wessel, a Norwegian mathematician and surveyor, publishes the first geometric representation of the complex numbers.

1801
Carl Friedrich Gauss, a German mathematician, publishes *Disquisitiones Arithmeticae.*

1805
Adrien-Marie Legendre, a French mathematician, publishes "Nouvelles méthodes pour la détermination des orbites des comètes," which contains the first description of the method of least squares.

1806
Jean-Robert Argand, a French bookkeeper, accountant, and mathematician, develops the Argand diagram to represent complex numbers.

1812
Pierre-Simon Laplace, a French mathematician, publishes *Théorie analytique des probabilités,* the most influential 19th-century work on the theory of probability.

1815
Napoléon suffers final defeat at the Battle of Waterloo.

Jean-Victor Poncelet, a French mathematician and "father of projective geometry," publishes *Traité des propriétés projectives des figures.*

1824

The French engineer Sadi Carnot publishes *Réflexions,* wherein he describes the Carnot engine.

Niels Henrik Abel, a Norwegian mathematician, publishes his proof of the impossibility of algebraically solving a general fifth-degree equation.

1826

Nikolay Ivanovich Lobachevsky, a Russian mathematician and "the Copernicus of geometry," announces his theory of non-Euclidean geometry.

1828

Robert Brown, a Scottish botanist, publishes the first description of Brownian motion in "A Brief Account of Microscopical Observations."

1830

Charles Babbage, a British mathematician and inventor, begins work on his analytical engine, the first attempt at a modern computer.

1832

János Bolyai, a Hungarian mathematician, publishes *Absolute Science of Space.*

The French mathematician Evariste Galois is killed in a duel.

1843

James Prescott Joule publishes his measurement of the mechanical equivalent of heat.

1846

The planet Neptune is discovered by the French mathematician Urbain-Jean-Joseph Le Verrier through a mathematical analysis of the orbit of Uranus.

1847

Georg Christian von Staudt publishes *Geometrie der Lage*, which shows that projective geometry can be expressed without any concept of length.

1848

Bernhard Bolzano, a Czech mathematician and theologian, dies. His study of infinite sets, *Paradoxien des Unendlichen*, is first published in 1851.

1850

Rudolph Clausius, a German mathematician and physicist, publishes his first paper on the theory of heat.

1851

William Thomson (Lord Kelvin), a British scientist, publishes "On the Dynamical Theory of Heat."

1854

George Boole, a British mathematician, publishes *Laws of Thought*. The mathematics contained therein later makes possible the design of computer logic circuits.

The German mathematician Bernhard Riemann gives a historic lecture, "On the Hypotheses That Form the Foundations of Geometry." The ideas therein later play an integral part in the theory of relativity.

1855

John Snow, a British physician, publishes "On the Mode of Communication of Cholera," the first successful epidemiological study of a disease.

1859

James Clerk Maxwell, a British physicist, proposes a probabilistic model for the distribution of molecular velocities in a gas.

Charles Darwin, a British biologist, publishes *On the Origin of Species by Means of Natural Selection*.

1861

The American Civil War begins.

1866

The Austrian biologist and monk Gregor Mendel publishes his ideas on the theory of heredity in "Versuche über Pflanzenhybriden."

1867

The Canadian Articles of Confederation unify the British colonies of North America.

1871

Otto von Bismarck is appointed first chancellor of the German Empire.

1872

The German mathematician Felix Klein announces his Erlanger Programm, an attempt to categorize all geometries with the use of group theory.

Lord Kelvin (William Thomson) develops an early analog computer to predict tides.

Richard Dedekind, a German mathematician, rigorously establishes the connection between real numbers and the real number line.

1874

Georg Cantor, a German mathematician, publishes "Über eine Eigenschaft des Inbegriffes aller reelen algebraischen Zahlen," a pioneering paper that shows that not all infinite sets are the same size.

1890

The Hollerith tabulator, an important innovation in calculating machines, is installed at the United States Census for use in the 1890 census.

1899

The German mathematician David Hilbert publishes the definitive axiomatic treatment of Euclidean geometry.

1900

David Hilbert announces his list of mathematics problems for the 20th century.

The Russian mathematician Andrey Andreyevich Markov begins his research into the theory of probability.

1901
Henri-Léon Lebesgue, a French mathematician, develops his theory of integration.

1905
Ernst Zermelo, a German mathematician, undertakes the task of axiomatizing set theory.

Albert Einstein, a German-born American physicist, begins to publish his discoveries in physics.

1906
Marian Smoluchowski, a Polish scientist, publishes his insights into Brownian motion.

1908
The Hardy-Weinberg law, containing ideas fundamental to population genetics, is published.

1910
Bertrand Russell, a British logician and philosopher, and Alfred North Whitehead, a British mathematician and philosopher, publish *Principia Mathematica*, an important work on the foundations of mathematics.

1914
World War I begins.

1917
Vladimir Ilyich Lenin leads a revolution that results in the founding of the Union of Soviet Socialist Republics.

1918
World War I ends.

The German mathematician Emmy Noether presents her ideas on the roles of symmetries in physics.

1929
Andrey Nikolayevich Kolmogorov, a Russian mathematician, publishes *General Theory of Measure and Probability Theory*, establishing the theory of probability on a firm axiomatic basis for the first time.

1930
Ronald Aylmer Fisher, a British geneticist and statistician, publishes *Genetical Theory of Natural Selection*, an important early attempt to express the theory of natural selection through mathematics.

1931
Kurt Gödel, an Austrian-born American mathematician, publishes his incompleteness proof.

The Differential Analyzer, an important development in analog computers, is developed at Massachusetts Institute of Technology

1933
Karl Pearson, a British innovator in statistics, retires from University College, London.

1935
George Horace Gallup, a U.S. statistician, founds the American Institute of Public Opinion.

1937
The British mathematician Alan Turing publishes his insights on the limits of computability.

1939
World War II begins.

William Edwards Deming joins the United States Census Bureau.

1945
World War II ends.

1946
The Electronic Numerical Integrator and Calculator (ENIAC) computer begins operation at the University of Pennsylvania.

1948

While working at Bell Telephone Labs in the United States, Claude Shannon publishes "A Mathematical Theory of Communication," marking the beginning of the Information Age.

1951

The Universal Automatic Computer (UNIVAC I) is installed at the U.S. Bureau of the Census.

1954

FORmula TRANslator (FORTRAN), one of the first high-level computer languages, is introduced.

1956

The American Walter Shewhart, innovator in the field of quality control, retires from Bell Telephone Laboratories.

1957

Olga Oleinik publishes "Discontinuous Solutions to Nonlinear Differential Equations," a milestone in mathematical physics.

1964

IBM Corporation introduces the IBM System/360 computer for government agencies and large businesses.

1965

Andrey Nikolayevich Kolmogorov establishes the branch of mathematics now known as Kolmogorov complexity.

1966

The A Programming Language (APL) is implemented on the IBM System/360 computer.

1972

Amid much fanfare, the French mathematician and philosopher René Thom establishes a new field of mathematics called catastrophe theory.

1973

The C computer language, developed at Bell Laboratories, is essentially completed.

1975

The French geophysicist Jean Morlet helps develop a new kind of analysis based on what he calls wavelets.

1977

Digital Equipment Corporation introduces the VAX computer.

1981

IBM Corporation introduces the IBM personal computer (PC).

1989

The Belgian mathematician Ingrid Daubechies develops what has become the mathematical foundation for today's wavelet research.

1991

The Union of Soviet Socialists Republics dissolves into 15 separate nations.

1995

The British mathematician Andrew Wiles publishes the first proof of Fermat's last theorem.

Cray Research introduces the CRAY E-1200, a machine that sustains a rate of 1 terraflop (1 trillion calculations per second) on real-world applications.

JAVA computer language is introduced commercially by Sun Microsystems.

1997

René Thom declares the mathematical field of catastrophe theory "dead."

2002

Experimental Mathematics celebrates its 10th anniversary. It is a refereed journal dedicated to the experimental aspects of mathematical research.

Manindra Agrawal, Neeraj Kayal, and Nitin Saxena create a brief, elegant algorithm to test whether a number is prime, thereby solving an important centuries-old problem.

2003

Grigory Perelman produces what may be the first complete proof of the Poincaré conjecture, a statement on the most fundamental properties of three-dimensional shapes.

GLOSSARY

algebra (1) a mathematical system that is a generalization of arithmetic, in which letters or other symbols are used to represent numbers; (2) the study of the formal relations between symbols belonging to sets on which one or more operations has been defined

algebraic equation an equation of the form $a_n x^n + a_{n-1} x^{n-1} + \ldots + a_1 x + a_0 = 0$ where n can represent any natural number, x represents the variable raised to the power indicated, and a_j, which always represents a rational number, is the coefficient by which x^j is multiplied

algorithm a formula or procedure used to solve a mathematical problem

analytic geometry the branch of mathematics that studies geometry via algebraic methods and coordinate systems

axiom a statement accepted as true that serves as a basis for deductive reasoning

characteristic equation an algebraic equation associated with the determinant of a given matrix with the additional property that the matrix acts as a root of the equation

coefficient a number or symbol representing a number used to multiply a variable

combinatorics the branch of mathematics concerned with the selection of elements from finite sets and the operations that are performed with those sets

commensurable evenly divisible by a common measure. Two lengths (or numbers representing those lengths) are commensurable when they are evenly divisible by a common unit

complex number any number of the form $a + bi$ where a and b are real numbers and i has the property that $i^2 = -1$

composite number a whole number greater than 1 that is not prime

conic section any member of the family of curves obtained from the intersection of a double cone and a plane

coordinate system a method of establishing a one-to-one correspondence between points in space and sets of numbers

deduction a conclusion obtained by logically reasoning from general principles to particular statements

degree of an equation for an algebraic equation of one variable, the largest exponent appearing in the equation

determinant a particular function defined on the set of square matrices. The value of the determinant is a real or complex number

determinant equation an equation or system of equations for which there exists a unique solution

eigenvalue the root of a characteristic equation

ellipse a closed curve formed by the intersection of a right circular cone and a plane

field a set of numbers with the property that however two numbers are combined via the operations of addition, subtraction, multiplication, and division (except by 0), the result is another number in the set

fifth-degree equation an algebraic equation in which the highest exponent appearing in the equation is 5

fourth-degree equation an algebraic equation in which the highest exponent appearing in the equation is 4

fundamental principle of analytic geometry the observation that under fairly general conditions one equation in two variables defines a curve

fundamental principle of solid analytic geometry the observation that under fairly general conditions one equation in three variables defines a surface

fundamental theorem of algebra the statement that any polynomial of degree n has n roots

geometric algebra a method of expressing ideas usually associated with algebra via the concepts and techniques of Euclidean geometry

group a set of objects together with an operation analogous to multiplication such that (1) the "product" of any two elements in the set is an element in the set; (2) the operation is associative, that is, for any three elements, a, b, and c in the group $(ab)c = a(bc)$; (3) there is an element in the set, usually denoted with the letter e, such that $ea = ae = a$ where a is any element in the set; and (4) every element in the set has an inverse, so that if a is an element in the set, there is an element called a^{-1} such that $aa^{-1} = e$

group theory the branch of mathematics devoted to the study of groups

hyperbola a curve composed of the intersection of a plane and both parts of a double, right circular cone

identity the element, usually denoted with the letter e, in a group with the property that if g is any element in the group, then $eg = ge = g$

indeterminate equation an equation or set of equations for which there exist infinitely many solutions

irrational number any real number that cannot be expressed as a/b, where a and b are integers and b is not 0

integer any whole number

linear equation an algebraic equation in which every term is a number or a variable of degree 1 multiplied by a number

matrix a rectangular array or table of numbers or other quantities

natural number the number 1, or any number obtained by adding 1 to itself sufficiently many times

one-to-one correspondence the pairing of elements between two sets, A and B, such that each element of A is paired with a unique element of B and to each element of B is paired a unique element of A

parabola the curve formed by the intersection of a right circular cone and a plane that is parallel to a line that generates the cone

polynomial a mathematical expression consisting of the sum of terms of the form ax^n, where a represents a number, x represents a variable, and n represents a nonnegative integer

prime number a natural number greater than 1 that is—among the set of all natural numbers—evenly divisible only by itself and 1

Pythagorean theorem the statement that for a right triangle the square of the length of the hypotenuse equals the sum of the squares of the lengths of the remaining sides

Pythagorean triple three numbers each of which is a natural number such that the sum of the squares of the two smaller numbers equals the square of the largest number.

quadratic equation See SECOND-DEGREE EQUATION

quadratic formula a mathematical formula for computing the roots of any second-degree algebraic equation by using the coefficients that appear in the equation

rational number any number of the form a/b, where a and b are integers and b is not 0

real number any rational number or any number that can be approximated to an arbitrarily high degree of accuracy by a rational number

rhetorical algebra algebra that is expressed in words only, without specialized algebraic symbols

root for any algebraic equation any number that satisfies the equation

second-degree equation an algebraic equation in which the highest exponent appearing in the equation is 2

spectral theory the study that seeks to relate the properties of a matrix to the properties of its eigenvalues

syllogism a type of formal logical argument described in detail by Aristotle in the collection of his writings known as *The Organon*

symmetry transformation a change, such as a rotation or reflection, of a geometric or physical object with the property that the spatial configuration of the object is the same before and after the transformation

syncopated algebra a method of expressing algebra that uses some abbreviations but does not employ a fully symbolic system of algebraic notation

third-degree equation an algebraic equation in which the highest exponent appearing in the equation is 3

unit fraction a fraction of the form $1/a$, where a is any integer except 0

FURTHER READING

MODERN WORKS

Adler, Irving. *Thinking Machines, a Layman's Introduction to Logic, Boolean Algebra, and Computers.* New York: John Day, 1961. This old book is still the best nontechnical introduction to computer arithmetic. It begins with fingers and ends with Boolean logic circuits.

Bashmakova, Izabella G. *The Beginnings and Evolution of Algebra.* Washington, D.C.: Mathematical Association of America, 2000. Aimed at older high school students, this is a detailed look at algebra from the age of Mesopotamia to the end of the 19th century. It presupposes a strong background in high school–level algebra.

Boyer, Carl B., and Uta C. Merzbach. *A History of Mathematics.* New York: John Wiley & Sons, 1991. Boyer was one of the preeminent mathematics historians of the 20th century. This work contains much interesting biographical information. The mathematical information assumes a fairly strong background of the reader.

Bruno, Leonard C. *Math and Mathematicians: The History of Mathematics Discoveries around the World,* 2 vols. Detroit: U.X.L, 1999. Despite its name there is little mathematics in this two-volume set. What you will find is a very large number of brief biographies of many individuals who were important in the history of mathematics.

Bunt, Lucas Nicolaas Hendrik, Phillip S. Jones, Jack D. Bedient. *The Historical Roots of Elementary Mathematics.* Englewood Cliffs, N.J.: Prentice-Hall, 1976. A highly detailed examination—complete with numerous exercises—of how ancient cultures added, subtracted, divided, multiplied, and reasoned.

Carroll, L. *Symbolic Logic and The Game of Logic.* New York: Dover Publications, 1958. Better known as the author of Alice in Wonderland, Lewis Carroll was also an accomplished mathematician. The language in these two books (bound as one) is old-fashioned but very accessible.

Courant, Richard, and Herbert Robbins. *What Is Mathematics? An Elementary Approach to Ideas and Mathematics.* New York: Oxford University Press, 1941. A classic and exhaustive answer to the question posed in the title. Courant was an influential 20th-century mathematician.

Danzig, Tobias. *Number, the Language of Science.* New York: Macmillan, 1954. First published in 1930, this book is painfully elitist; the author's many prejudices are on display in every chapter. Yet it is one of the best nontechnical histories of the concept of number ever written. Apparently it was also Albert Einstein's favorite book on the history of mathematics.

Dewdney, Alexander K. *200% of Nothing: An Eye-Opening Tour through the Twists and Turns of Math Abuse and Innumeracy.* New York: John Wiley & Sons, 1993. A critical look at how mathematical reasoning has been abused to distort truth.

Eastaway, Robert, and Jeremy Wyndham. *Why Do Buses Come in Threes? The Hidden Mathematics of Everyday Life.* New York: John Wiley & Sons, 1998. Nineteen lighthearted essays on the mathematics underlying everything from luck to scheduling problems.

Eves, Howard. *An Introduction to the History of Mathematics.* New York: Holt, Rinehart & Winston, 1953. This well-written history of mathematics places special emphasis on early mathematics. It is unusual because the history is accompanied by numerous mathematical problems. (The solutions are in the back of the book.)

Freudenthal, Hans. *Mathematics Observed.* New York: McGraw-Hill, 1967. A collection of seven survey articles about math topics from computability to geometry to physics (some more technical than others).

Gardner, Martin. *The Colossal Book of Mathematics.* New York: Norton, 2001. Martin Gardner had a gift for seeing things mathematically. This "colossal" book contains sections on geometry, algebra, probability, logic, and more.

————. *Logic Machines and Diagrams.* Chicago: University of Chicago Press, 1982. An excellent book on logic and its uses in computers.

Guillen, Michael. *Bridges to Infinity: The Human Side of Mathematics.* Los Angeles: Jeremy P. Tarcher, 1983. This book consists of an engaging nontechnical set of essays on mathematical topics, including non-Euclidean geometry, transfinite numbers, and catastrophe theory.

Heath, Thomas L. *A History of Greek Mathematics.* New York: Dover Publications, 1981. First published early in the 20th century and reprinted numerous times, this book is still one of the main references on the subject.

Hoffman, Paul. *Archimedes' Revenge: The Joys and Perils of Mathematics.* New York: Ballantine, 1989. A relaxed, sometimes silly look at an interesting and diverse set of math problems ranging from prime numbers and cryptography to Turing machines and the mathematics of democratic processes.

Hogben, L. *Mathematics for the Million.* New York: W. W. Norton, 1968. This is a classic text that has been in print for many decades. Written by a creative scientist, it reveals a view of mathematics, its history, and its applications that is both challenging and entertaining. Highly recommended.

Jacquette, D. *On Boole.* Belmont, Calif.: Wadsworth/Thompson Learning, 2002. This book gives a good overview of Aristotelian syllogisms, Boolean algebra, and the uses of Boolean algebra in the design of computer logic circuits.

Joseph, George G. *The Crest of the Peacock: The Non-European Roots of Mathematics.* Princeton, N.J.: Princeton University Press, 1991. One of the best of a new crop of books devoted to this important topic.

Keyser, Cassius J. The Group Concept. In *The World of Mathematics*, vol. 3, edited by James R. Newman. New York: Dover Publications, 1956. A nice introduction to the theory of groups that does not depend on previous experience with higher mathematics.

Kline, Morris. *Mathematics and the Physical World.* New York: Thomas Y. Crowell, 1959. The history of mathematics as it relates to the history of science, and vice versa.

———. *Mathematics for the Nonmathematician.* New York: Dover Publications, 1985. An articulate, not very technical overview of many important mathematical ideas.

———. *Mathematics in Western Culture.* New York: Oxford University Press, 1953. An excellent overview of the development of Western mathematics in its cultural context, this book is aimed at an audience with a firm grasp of high school–level mathematics.

McLeish, John. *Number.* New York: Fawcett Columbine, 1992. A history of the concept of number from Mesopotamia to modern times.

Pappas, Theoni. *The Joy of Mathematics.* San Carlos, Calif.: World Wide/Tetra, 1986. Aimed at a younger audience, this work searches for interesting applications of mathematics in the world around us.

Pierce, John R. *An Introduction to Information Theory: Symbols, Signals and Noise.* New York: Dover Publications, 1961. Despite the sound of the title, this is not a textbook. Among other topics, Pierce, formerly of Bell Laboratories, describes some of the mathematics involved in encoding numbers and text for digital transmission or storage—a lucid introduction to the topics of information and algebraic coding theory.

Reid, Constance. *From Zero to Infinity: What Makes Numbers Interesting.* New York: Thomas Y. Crowell, 1960. A well-written overview of numbers and the algebra that stimulated their development.

Sawyer, Walter. *What Is Calculus About?* New York: Random House, 1961. A highly readable description of a sometimes-intimidating, historically important subject. Absolutely no calculus background required.

Schiffer, M. and Leon Bowden. *The Role of Mathematics in Science.* Washington, D.C.: Mathematical Association of America, 1984. The first few chapters of this book, ostensibly written for high school students, will be accessible to many students; the last few chapters will find a much narrower audience.

Smith, David E., and Yoshio Mikami. *A History of Japanese Mathematics.* Chicago: Open Court, 1914. Copies of this book are still around, and it is frequently quoted. The first half is an informative nontechnical survey. The second half is written more for the expert.

Stewart, Ian. *From Here to Infinity.* New York: Oxford University Press, 1996. A well-written, very readable overview of several important contemporary ideas in geometry, algebra, computability, chaos, and mathematics in nature.

Swetz, Frank J., editor. *From Five Fingers to Infinity: A Journey through the History of Mathematics.* Chicago: Open Court, 1994. This is a fascinating, though not especially focused, look at the history of mathematics. Highly recommended.

Swetz, Frank. *Sea Island Mathematical Manual: Surveying and Mathematics in Ancient China.* University Park: Pennsylvania State University Press, 1992. The book contains many ancient problems in mathematics and measurement and illustrates how problems in measurement often inspired the development of geometric ideas and techniques.

Tabak, John. *Numbers: Computers, Philosophers, and the Search for Meaning.* New York: Facts On File, 2004. More information about how the concept of number and ideas about the nature of algebra evolved together.

Thomas, David A. *Math Projects for Young Scientists.* New York: Franklin Watts, 1988. This project-oriented text is an introduction to several historically important geometry problems.

Yaglom, Isaac M. *Geometric Transformations,* translated by Allen Shields. New York: Random House, 1962. Aimed at high school students, this is a very sophisticated treatment of "simple" geometry and an excellent introduction to higher mathematics. It is also an excellent introduction to the concept of invariance.

Zippin, Leo. *The Uses of Infinity.* New York: Random House, 1962. Contains lots of equations—perhaps too many for the uninitiated—but none of the equations is very difficult. The book is worth the effort required to read it.

ORIGINAL SOURCES

It can sometimes deepen our appreciation of an important mathematical discovery to read the discoverer's own description. Often this is not possible, because the description is too technical. Fortunately there are exceptions. Sometimes the discovery is accessible because the idea does not require a lot of technical background to appreciate it. Sometimes the discoverer writes a nontechnical account of the technical idea that she or he has discovered. Here are some classic papers:

Ahmes. *The Rhind Mathematical Papyrus: Free Translation, Commentary, and Selected Photographs, Transcription, Literal Translations*, translated by Arnold B. Chace. Reston, Va.: National Council of Teachers of Mathematics, 1979. This is a translation of the biggest and best of extant Egyptian mathematical texts, the Rhind papyrus (also known as the Ahmes papyrus). It provides insight into the types of problems and methods of solution known to one of humanity's oldest cultures.

Boole, George. *Mathematical Analysis of Logic*. In *The World of Mathematics*, vol. 3, edited by James R. Newman. New York: Dover Publications, 1956. This is a nontechnical excerpt from one of Boole's most famous works. Although there is no "Boolean algebra" in this article, it contains Boole's own explanation for what he hoped to gain from studying the laws of thought.

Descartes, René. *The Geometry*. In *The World of Mathematics*, vol. 1, edited by James Newman. New York: Dover Publications, 1956. This is a readable translation of an excerpt from Descartes's own revolutionary work *La Géométrie*.

Euclid. *Elements*. Translated by Sir Thomas L. Heath. *Great Books of the Western World*. Vol. 11. Chicago: Encyclopaedia Britannica, 1952. See especially book I for Euclid's own exposition of the axiomatic method, and read some of the early propositions in this volume to see how the Greeks investigated mathematics without equations.

Galilei, Galileo. *Dialogues Concerning Two New Sciences*. Translated by Henry Crew and Alfonso de Salvio. New York: Dover Publications,

1954. An interesting literary work as well as a pioneering physics text. Many regard the publication of this text as the beginning of the modern scientific tradition.

Hardy, Godfrey H. *A Mathematician's Apology*. Cambridge, England: Cambridge University Press, 1940. Hardy was an excellent mathematician and a good writer. In this oft-quoted and very brief book Hardy seeks to explain and sometimes justify his life as a mathematician.

Russell, Bertrand. *Mathematics and the Metaphysicians*. In *The World of Mathematics*. Vol. 3, edited by James Newman. New York: Dover Publications, 1956. An introduction to the philosophical ideas upon which mathematics is founded written by a major contributor to this field.

INTERNET RESOURCES

Athena Earth and Space Science for K–12. Available on-line. URL: http://inspire.ospi.wednet.edu:8001/. Updated May 13, 1999. Funded by NASA's Public Use of Remote Sensing Data, this site contains many interesting applications of mathematics to the study of natural phenomena.

Boyne, Anne. Papers on History of Science. http://nti.educa. rcanaria.es/penelope/uk_confboye.htm#particular. Downloaded June 2, 2003. This is a very detailed and interesting paper devoted to the history of negative numbers. It is well worth reading.

The Eisenhower National Clearinghouse for Mathematics and Science Education. Available on-line. URL: http://www.enc.org/. Downloaded on June 2, 2003. As its name implies, this site is a "clearinghouse" for a comprehensive set of links to interesting sites in math and science.

Electronic Bookshelf. Available on-line. URL: http://hilbert. dartmouth.edu/~matc/eBookshelf/art/index.html. Updated on May 21, 2002. This site is maintained by Dartmouth College. It is both visually beautiful and informative, and it has links to many creative presentations on computer science, the history of mathematics, and mathematics. It also treats a number of other topics from a mathematical perspective.

Eric Weisstein's World of Mathematics. Available on-line. URL: http://mathworld.wolfram.com/. Updated on April 10, 2002. This site has brief overviews of a great many topics in mathematics. The level of presentation varies substantially from topic to topic.

Faber, Vance, et al. This is MEGA Mathematics! Available on-line. URL: http://www.c3.lanl.gov/mega-math. Downloaded June 2, 2003. Maintained by the Los Alamos National Laboratories, one of the premier scientific establishments in the world, this site has a number of unusual offerings. It is well worth a visit.

Fife, Earl, and Larry Husch. Math Archives. "History of Mathematics." Available on-line. URL: http://archives.math.utk. edu/topics/history.html. Updated January 2002. Information on mathematics, mathematicians, and mathematical organizations.

Gangolli, Ramesh. *Asian Contributions to Mathematics.* Available on-line. URL: http://www.pps.k12.or.us/depts-c/mc-me/be-as-ma.pdf. Downloaded on June 2, 2003. As its name implies, this well-written on-line book focuses on the history of mathematics in Asia and its effect on the world history of mathematics. It also includes information on the work of Asian Americans, a welcome contribution to the field.

Heinlow, Lance, and Karen Pagel. "Math History." Online Resource. Available on-line. URL: http://www.amatyc.org/OnlineResource/index.html. Updated May 14, 2003. Created under the auspices of the American Mathematical Association of Two-Year Colleges, this site is a very extensive collection of links to mathematical and math-related topics.

Howard, Mike. *Introduction to Crystallography and Mineral Crystal Systems.* Available on-line. URL: http://www.rockhounds. com/rockshop/xtal/. Downloaded June 3, 2003. The author has designed a nice introduction to the use of group theory in the study of crystals through an interesting mix of geometry, algebra, and mineralogy.

The Math Forum @ Drexel. The Math Forum Student Center. Available on-line. URL: http://mathforum.org/students/. Updated June 2, 2003. Probably the best website for information about the kinds of mathematics that students encounter in their school-related studies. You will find interesting and challenging problems and solutions for students in grades K–12 as well as a fair amount of college-level information.

Melville, Duncan J. Mesopotamian Mathematics. Available on-line. URL: http://it.stlawu.edu/ca.dmelvill/mesomath/. Updated March 17, 2003. This creative site is devoted to many aspects of Mesopotamian mathematics. It also has a link to a "cuneiform calculator," which can be fun to use.

O'Connor, John L., and Edmund F. Robertson. The MacTutor History of Mathematics Archive. Available on-line. URL: http://www.gap.dcs.st-and.ac.uk/~history/index.html. Updated May 2003. This is a valuable resource for anyone interested in learning more about the history of mathematics. It contains an extraordinary collection of biographies of mathematicians in different cultures and times. In addition it provides information about the historical development of certain key mathematical ideas.

PERIODICALS, THROUGH THE MAIL AND ON-LINE

+Plus

URL: http://pass.maths.org.uk
A site with numerous interesting articles about all aspects of high school math. They send an email every few weeks to their subscribers to keep them informed about new articles at the site.

Function

Business Manager
Department of Mathematics and Statistics
Monash University
Victoria 3800
Australia

function@maths.monash.edu.au
Published five times per year, this refereed journal is aimed at older high school students.

The Math Goodies Newsletter

http://www.mathgoodies.com/newsletter/
A popular, free e-newsletter that is sent out twice per month.

Parabola: A Mathematics Magazine for Secondary Students

Australian Mathematics Trust
University of Canberra
ACT 2601
Australia
Published twice a year by the Australian Mathematics Trust in association with the University of New South Wales, *Parabola* is a source of short high-quality articles on many aspects of mathematics. Some back issues are also available free on-line. See URL: http://www.maths.unsw.edu.au/Parabola/index.html.

Pi in the Sky

http://www.pims.math.ca/pi/
Part of the Pacific Institute for the Mathematical Sciences, this high school mathematics magazine is available over the Internet.

Scientific American

415 Madison Avenue
New York, NY 10017
A serious and widely read monthly magazine, *Scientific American* regularly carries high-quality articles on mathematics and mathematically intensive branches of science. This is the one "popular" source of high-quality mathematical information that you will find at a newsstand.

INDEX

Italic page numbers indicate illustrations.